THE BOLD ALTERNATIVE

THE BOLD ALTERNATIVE

Staying in Church in the 21st Century

Gary W. Charles

GENEVA

Geneva Press
Louisville, Kentucky

Book design by Sharon Adams
Cover design by Cat & Mouse Design

First edition
Published by Geneva Press
Louisville, Kentucky

This book is printed on acid-free paper that meets the American National Standards Institute Z39.48 standard.♾

PRINTED IN THE UNITED STATES OF AMERICA

01 02 03 04 05 06 07 08 09 10 — 10 9 8 7 6 5 4 3 2 1

Library of Congress Cataloging-in-Publication Data

A catalog record for this book may be obtained from the Library of Congress.
ISBN 0-664-50179-6

For Jennell

Contents

Preface

My sincere thanks to the Louisville Institute, the members of the Old Presbyterian Meeting House, the staff with whom I am most fortunate to serve, and to Jennell, Erin, and Joshua for their patient and loving support of this study. With the guidance of mentors Louis B. Weeks, President of Union Theological Seminary and Presbyterian School of Christian Education in Richmond, Virginia; Loren Mead, founder of the Alban Institute; William R. Phillippe, former Parish Associate at the Old Presbyterian Meeting House in Alexandria, Virginia; Burton Newman, a Presbyterian pastor recently retired and the Continuing Education Coordinator at Virginia Theological Seminary; and Thomas G. Long, Professor of Preaching at Candler School of Theology and Senior Editorial Consultant for Geneva Press, I selected six vibrant and vital Presbyterian congregations in the Presbyterian Church (U.S.A). In each one, I sat at the feet of faithful members and leaders and tried to discern God's Spirit at work in the church today.

The criteria for identifying a Presbyterian congregation as vital and vibrant included the following:

1. The congregation's membership includes sufficient members in each of the proposed focus groups: Group 1—lifelong Presbyterians, Group 2—lifelong Christians, now Presbyterians, Group 3—new Christians/Presbyterians.

2. The congregation has a stated commitment to corporate worship as being central to the church's life.
3. Attendance in corporate worship has been growing over the past five years.
4. Pastoral and lay leadership is strong and the congregation is not dominated by one powerful member or pastor.
5. The budget is ambitious and is consistently met without an over-dependence on endowments or a few wealthy patrons.
6. The educational program offers innovative approaches to equip the laity for ministry.
7. The mission of the congregation finds strong expressions within the local community, as well as nationally and globally.
8. The leadership, lay and ordained, embraces the Reformed theological heritage while being open to exploring new worship practices, theological developments, and ministry practices in this postmodern era of the church.
9. The leaders within the congregation encourage and maintain an openness to church participation and membership, sensitive not to exclude those persons who often have been excluded both by society and the church.

I was fortunate to get the enthusiastic support and participation of the following congregations and their pastors: Laird Stuart and the Calvary Presbyterian Church in San Francisco; Thomas Tewell and the Fifth Avenue Presbyterian Church in New York City; John Buchanan and John Wilkinson and the Fourth Presbyterian Church in Chicago; Theodore Wardlaw and the Central Presbyterian Church in Atlanta; Stuart Broberg and Leslie Klingensmith and the Westminster Presbyterian Church in Alexandria, Virginia; and Arthur Ross and the White Memorial Presbyterian Church in Raleigh, North Carolina.

Over a six-month period, I made a site visit to each of these congregations and conducted focus group interviews with the three groups listed in the first criterion above. I am deeply indebted to Stephanie Horowitz for her faithful transcription of these interviews. In advance of my visit, I sent the participants a letter of introduction that outlined the purpose of the study and also a written questionnaire (see Appendix A).

While at the participating congregations, I interviewed each of the three focus groups for a ninety-minute period. The focus group interview followed a format of ten questions (see Appendix B) intended to reveal how active members of vital and vibrant Presbyterian congregations understand the Presbyterian theological tradition, the nature and purpose of the church today, corporate worship, spirituality, Christian vocation, and the mission of the church in a secular and pluralistic culture. It is the voices of these participants, both pastors and laity, that are heard throughout this book, though I have used pseudonyms for each quotation to respect the privacy of the participants. Pastors were asked not to participate in the focus groups, so as not to prejudice the participants' answers. All gladly honored my request.

This book is the result of the vision for ministry I gained from committed believers and congregations throughout the land. Their voices need to be heard in a wider forum. I am deeply indebted to Fred Morhart, Louis B. Weeks, and Tom Long, who have read each chapter and told me ever so kindly to work some more.

Acknowledgments

Grateful acknowledgment is made to the following for permission to quote copyrighted material:

Augsburg Fortress, from Douglas John Hall, *Why Christian? For Those on the Edge of Faith,* copyright © 1998 Augsburg Fortress.

Wm. B. Eerdmans Publishing Co., from Nile Harper, *Urban Churches, Vital Signs,* © 1999 Wm. B. Eerdmans Publishing Co., Grand Rapids, Michigan. All rights reserved.

Hodder & Stoughton Ltd, from Norman Shanks, *Iona—God's Energy: The Vision and Spirituality of the Iona Community,* copyright 1999.

Princeton University Press, from Robert Wuthnow, *The Restructuring of American Religion,* © 1988 by Princeton University Press; and from Wade Clark Roof, *Spiritual Marketplace: Baby Boomers and the Remaking of American Religion,* © 1999 by Princeton University Press.

University of California Press, from Robert Wuthnow, *After Heaven: Spirituality in America since the 1950s.* Copyright © 1998.

Westminster John Knox Press, from Milton J. Coalter, John M. Mulder, and Louis B. Weeks, eds, *The Re-Forming Tradition,* © 1992 Westminster/John Knox Press.

Chapter 1

Why They Come

On any given Sunday, vast numbers of Americans do not darken the door of any church. This book is not about them. Instead, in the following pages, you will hear from people who, regardless of their age, denominational background, or time since their baptism and profession of faith, worship on most Sundays of the year. They also prepare bag lunches, sing in choirs, put checks in the offering plate, spend the night at homeless shelters, lead advocacy groups for those whom society neglects, teach biblical interpretation to peer-pressured youth, and spend countless hours in committee meetings.

John Buchanan, pastor of the Fourth Presbyterian Church in Chicago and editor of *The Christian Century,* observes: "Week after week, in every community in our nation, Christians engage in countercultural, and a sometimes culturally subversive, activity: they gather in their churches to affirm their belief in God, to pray and think together about what it means to live in God's world as God's children, and to give generously of their lives and resources to support the work they believe God wants done in the world."[1]

But why do people make the increasingly unlikely choice to come to church when so many Americans, especially in urban areas, do not?

Ted, a lifelong Christian in Alexandria, Virginia, who has found a home in several denominations, said: "You've got to have something more in your life on Sunday morning than Starbucks and *The Washington Post.*"

Melissa, a newly baptized young adult in San Francisco, explained: "It ends my week and begins my week. Even though I have my own scriptural and prayer life at home, it just isn't the same. I need this community very much."

Jim, a young Christian in Atlanta, made this bold claim: "Church is one of the most hopeful public experiences of life. Watching people come in and realizing that these people are well-educated and powerful. They've got all kinds of things they could be doing with their time—but they are here. This is where our hope is, individually and collectively."

The voices in this book are largely those of active churchgoers who worship and live amid the economic prosperity of contemporary America. These church members are acquainted with homelessness, unemployment, and suffocating debt, but mostly from the perspective of providing shelters and counseling and guidance. Most current mainline churchgoers live comfortably in a society that paints reality an unmistakable shade of green. One's assets and one's value as a person are often inextricably intertwined. Not only do market realities pronounce that people deserve success; they then measure success by what people accumulate, cite on their résumés, and drive onto congested city streets.

Sociologist Wade Clark Roof describes a growing uneasiness with this market identity ethos among active churchgoers: "Even among those lacking a good vocabulary for expressing their inner selves, or for whom spirituality is vaguely defined and without much real power to challenge their secular values and assumptions, there is a yearning for something that transcends a consumption ethic and material definitions of success."[2] Elias, a young member of Central Presbyterian Church in Atlanta, caught in the corporate achievement stream, reflected: "Sunday in church you are presented with an alternative. A lot of what you face during the week is pretty convincing—the advertisements, societal pressures, work pressures, all that. And church gives you a strong, consistent reminder of an alternative reality, an alternative way of being in the world." Like Elias, numerous young, new Christians, active in congregations across America tell poignant stories of coming to church to encounter an alternative reality to the seductive market and acquisitive trends so prevalent in the current culture. These Christians sit in sometimes sparsely attended sanctuaries hoping to find something more sustaining than a cup of coffee and the Sunday paper, anxious to be a part of one of the most hopeful public experiences of life, eager for a reality check, and committed to address a real void in their lives.

Speaking for a generation schooled by the often addictive, ceaseless, and consumptive habits of baby boomers, Laura, a Generation X Christian from Atlanta, mused: "You can easily become your environment, and there are lots of things I don't want to become." Convinced that the pervasive messages in American cultural and social life offer too shallow and narcissistic a definition of success, the concerns especially of young, urban Christians sound a recurring biblical theme. They issue a warning as did Amos to the financially affluent and morally bankrupt northern kingdom of Israel: "Alas for those who lie on beds of ivory, and lounge on their couches, and eat lambs from the flock, and calves from the stall; who sing idle songs to the sound of the harp, and like David improvise on instruments of music; who drink wine from bowls, and anoint themselves with the finest oils, but are not grieved over the ruin of Joseph! Therefore they shall now be the first to go into exile, and the revelry of the loungers shall pass away" (Amos 6:4–7 NRSV).

Remarkably, many young urban "success stories" come to church looking for a more authentic and altruistic environment than the one in which they work and live. With dramatic wealth created by the technological revolution and by an extended bull market, some churchgoers today find "success" at an early age. They reach "financial nirvana," only to learn that the promised contentment, fulfillment, and joy of being rich are less than that promised by the glossy posters and slick advertisements. Some people today, then, come to church looking to reevaluate the meaning of success. Many come prepared to lay claim to a very different vision of the good life: "He has told you, O mortal, what is good; and what does the LORD require of you but to do justice, and to love kindness, and to walk humbly with your God?" (Micah 6:8 NRSV). Sounding like a modern Micah, Duane, a young Christian in San Francisco, said: "I come to church because it keeps me grounded in what I believe. It's a challenge to remember what your core values are and what this is all about."

Many educated professionals who fill church pews today come looking to hear genuine words of truth. They come weary of what passes for "truth" in advertising, film, music, the print media, public discourse, and everyday conversation. They also come exhausted by the moral shortcuts required of them in the work place. Laird Stuart, pastor of Calvary Presbyterian Church in San Francisco, commented on the young people who attend there: "They have a low threshold for phoniness, because they face it everywhere they turn." Roof comments on this search for truth: "A post-traditional world of increased pluralism, relativism, and tolerance virtually assures a shift of perspective on truth and ontological certainty."[3]

In addition to a hunger for "unspun" truth, many churchgoers come with a thirst for something more nourishing than the current culture's philosophical fast food and more enduring than the advice of the latest self-help guru. They are suspicious, though, of shallow and hypocritical "church talk" and they come with questions about what the Bible can mean to a thinking person. Gerald, in Chicago, said: "I'm a Christian today because a preacher had the courage to interpret the biblical texts beyond the literalism of my childhood. Suddenly, God and Jesus and the ways of the kingdom made sense like they never did when I had to check my mind at the door." With bright and often unchurched young people sometimes venturing into congregations, churches that resist the urge to biblical and moral oversimplification find that some reluctant inquirers come again.

Though written years ago in different political and socioeconomic circumstances, Second Isaiah ends with a distinctly modern ring: "Ho, everyone who thirsts, come to the waters; and you that have no money, come, buy and eat! . . . Why do you spend your money for that which is not bread, and your labor for that which does not satisfy? Listen carefully to me, and eat what is good, and delight yourselves in rich food" (Isa. 55:1–2 NRSV). People, especially young people, come to church today because they live and work in a society that bloats their stomachs, pads their bank accounts, and jams their attics and garages, but often empties their minds and starves their souls. They come to church to hear words that carry with them comfort and challenge, judgment and grace, longing and hope. They come to eat a diet of rich food that will satisfy the fiercest spiritual and intellectual hunger of contemporary America.

More than ever before in American religious life, some people, especially the young, come to church despite a myriad of family obstacles. "My parents don't go to church at all," said Nadia, a new Christian in Chicago. "My mother considers it 'a corruption of character,' because we should be able to rely on ourselves. And I have recently decided that that is not really a practical way to go about life, because if I'm the only thing that matters, then my life is going nowhere." In group interviews nationwide, churchgoers tell stories of professions of faith that are often only tolerated, and more likely are belittled, by members of the immediate family. These church members understand well the Lord's warning in Luke: "Do you think that I have come to bring peace to the earth? No, I tell you, but rather division! From now on five in one household will be divided, three against two and two against three; they will be divided," he said,

> father against son
>   and son against father,
> mother against daughter
>   and daughter against mother,
> mother-in-law against her daughter-in-law
>   and daughter-in-law against her mother-in-law.
>   (Luke 12:51–53 NRSV)

In addition to obstacles from the family, people of all ages come to church today despite the demands of the job. The secularization of society and the demands of a booming economy have left employees with a difficult choice, rarely faced before by worshipers in America. As businesses expand to operate on a 24-hour, seven-day-a-week schedule, workers who choose to worship on Sunday and participate in weekday congregational activities are often viewed by their employers as liabilities, are treated as nuisances, and are denied advancements available to more "flexible" employees. Frances, a lifelong Christian in New York City, recounts a common choice that active Christians must make in the work force today: "I had to set boundaries when my vocation tried to infringe on my faith just because I work around the clock and often on weekends. I was asked to work on Sundays and I said, 'I go to church from 11 A.M. to noon on Sundays, and I would actually rather not work on the Sabbath at all.' I had to have a full meeting of my department to defend my attending religious services on Sunday."

As the mythology of a Christian America vaporizes into secular particles,[4] churchgoers are finding that a previously painless choice is no longer without pain or risk. Not too many years ago in the United States, church participation and economic advancement often complemented each other. Increasingly, however, the opposite is true, as women and men are forced to choose between church commitments and the relentless demands of a "24-7" world economy.

Yet people still come to church despite negative pressures from family, job, and society. Ralph, a new resident of North Carolina and a recently baptized Christian in the White Memorial Presbyterian Church in Raleigh, offers a moving description of why some people make the increasingly less likely choice to come to church today: "I would be a good before and after. I've got two kids and my wife and I got so caught up working and raising a family that Sunday was our day to flake out. But over time, there was a real void there and I think it took me a while to figure out that my faith was missing. You attain all the other goals. You set financial goals, move into a new house and buy a better car. We finally realized that faith was missing. I decided that I would try to raise my sons in a different manner than the way my parents introduced us to church."

A catechism for Reformed Christians (paraphrased here) asks: "What is the chief end of human life?" The response is: "To glorify God and revel in God's love and mercy forever." People defy many modern obstacles and come to church because their fundamental need to be in relationship with the living God has not changed over time despite drastic changes in the American religious and cultural landscapes. Listen to active Christians express this fundamental need in a variety of voices:

What brought me back to church was that I needed a place to give thanks to God on a regular basis.

I come to church to feel God's presence and to learn things that will help me go out and hopefully be somebody who can share that feeling with somebody else.

For me, it's very important to spend at least one day each week in worship, in appreciation to God for who God is and what God has done.

I come because I need to be here. It's very centering. I find myself here. If I don't show up for a week or so, I feel a little lost.

I come to be reminded of what I really need to be attending to.

Fewer people now attend mainline churches than in our country's recent past,[5] but those who come do so at a considerable cost, with decided commitment and great expectations of and for the church.

Not long ago in America's religious past, habit and guilt were major motivators for coming to church. Vestiges of habit or guilt sometimes still lead people to come to church, but they no longer hold enough sway to cause people to stay. In most mainline denominations, I suspect, fewer worshipers than ever before come to church simply out of habit or guilt. Todd, a young Presbyterian from Raleigh, reflected: "The habit gets you there, but I don't think it's really the reason you keep going. It's something you enjoy or you'd find a reason not to be there." Meredith, a new Christian in Atlanta, described a positive role for habit, but less as a motivator to come to church and more as a discipline to stay. She said: "I come to church out of routine now. If I don't do it, then even if I say, 'Oh, I'll spend an hour praying or I'll take the time during the week,' I won't do it." Since we live in a culture that deemphasizes and is mostly oblivious to church attendance and that regularly spreads a Sunday buffet of delightful temptations before its citizenry, habit no longer motivates many people to spend an active life in the church. Lifelong Christians and churchgoers still cite habit as a cause for coming to church, but even a majority of them recognize the diminished motivation of habit in a society that only tolerates and rarely rewards such behavior.

Guilt still motivates some people to attend church. Yet, especially in anonymous urban cultural milieus, where pressure to participate in church life is noticeably lacking, guilt languishes as a relatively impotent motivator. Sarah, a lifetime member of her congregation in Atlanta, echoed a common response from participants nationwide when asked about guilt as a motivator: "I don't really feel guilty when I'm not here. It's more that I miss the joy and the grace." On the other hand, Cleve, from the same congregation, suggested that guilt, like habit, can serve as an essential religious discipline. He gave three reasons for coming to church, one of which was guilt: "Guilt, in the sense that the least I can do is take an hour out of my Sunday morning to give thanks to God. Sure, it's my weekend. Sure, I've been working hard all week. Well, if I didn't have that job that God has given me the skills to do and if I didn't have all the things I do, where would I be?" Though still emphasized within some Christian traditions, both guilt and habit play diminishing roles in why people come to church today.

Art Ross, pastor of the White Memorial Presbyterian Church in Raleigh, North Carolina, contends: "I'm convinced that everybody that joins this church has some faith commitment. I think everybody is involved in a search and I believe that God is part of that search and that the community of God's people is part of that search." Habit, guilt, family and social expectations still lead some to church on Sunday mornings, particularly given certain demographic and ethnic factors.[6] However, increasingly, people come to church less for these reasons and more as an intentional choice, a deliberate exploration for purpose and meaning, and a bold expression of faith and hope.

Clearly, many of those who come to church today do so wishing to make a difference in the world. Erik, a corporate executive from Alexandria, stressed that he comes to church "for the opportunity it affords to do good for the community and for people in need, an opportunity I don't get in my job." A wise scribe once said to Jesus, "Teacher, you have truly said that 'God is one, and besides God there is no other,' and 'to love God with all the heart, and with all the understanding, and with all the strength,' and 'to love one's neighbor as oneself'—this is much more important than all whole burnt offerings and sacrifices." When Jesus saw that he answered wisely, he said to him, "You are not far from the kingdom of God" (Mark 12:28–34, au. trans.). People come to church today to join with those who seek to love their neighbors, whether serving Meals on Heels at the Fifth Avenue Church in New York City or tutoring in the nationally acclaimed education program of the Fourth Presbyterian Church in Chicago at the Cabrini-Green and Henry Horner housing projects. Serving as Stephen Ministers, reading scripture and praying with residents in nursing homes, passing petitions to curb gun sales and to stop the death penalty, they come to follow both the works and words of Jesus.

From newly baptized adults to those who have spent a lifetime in the church, perhaps more than ever before, people come to church today because they recognize the limits of unchecked individualism. Early in his ministry, Jesus called together diverse individuals as a community to travel and learn and worship with him. And long before Jesus, from the earliest days of Israel, through the tribal confederation and the years of the monarchy, during the exilic and postexilic period, the Bible tells about individuals who worked out their faith within a believing community. Ellie, a new member of her congregation in Chicago, echoed this biblical insight: "The Christian life is to be lived in community, not in isolation." Matt, who recently returned to church life in

Atlanta, confessed: "I fell away from church for some years. What brought me back was the feeling that I had to be worshiping with other people. Corporate worship—that's what started me back." Alexa, another person who has found her way back into the church in San Francisco, said: "This particular community of people, what we do at this church, what we stand for here; the corporate group ethos of it is what I need. I can give but I also get fed."

In his contemporary Christian apologetic *Why Christian?* Douglas John Hall gives a theological perspective on the importance of being in Christian community. He writes: "The necessity of the church can be expressed positively in at least three ways. It is necessary first of all because faith 'seeks understanding,' [and faith] also seeks *koinonia* (communion with others, participation). . . . There is something in faith—even in its initial stirrings, even when it may consist more of questions than of answers—that drives one to seek out others." In addition to a Christian's need for koinonia to explore the faith, Hall also argues for the role a Christian community can play as a milieu for the redemptive message of the gospel. He writes: "If reconciliation is what the Christian message is all about, and if there is any truth in that message, then it must express itself in a gathering of people who are reconciled to one another—or are at least beginning to be."[7]

A growing number of people fill the pews because they know the futility of "flying solo" in the Christian faith and sense the need for koinonia.[8] In Atlanta, Elyce, a longtime Christian believer but new to church participation, discovered a whole new dimension of her faith when she joined a congregation: "I've always had a close relationship with God, but I never really realized the value of going to church and what that would instill in your life until I joined here." Through her church participation, Elyce uncovered levels of her faith never realized in her solo pursuits. The limitations of a Christian life lived in isolation and the essential need for a community recalls the simple wisdom of Paul as he wrote to the contentious Corinthians: "The body does not consist of one member but of many. . . . Now you are the body of Christ and individually members of it" (1 Cor. 12:14, 27 NRSV).

Mary, a recently baptized college professor in Chicago, gave one of the most compelling witnesses for coming to church. She cited the potentially transforming importance of a welcoming and loving body of Christ. Mary described her lifelong antipathy toward the church and her condescension toward those who professed faith in God. A friend convinced her to attend a choral service at Fourth Presbyterian on Good Friday: "I was so anti-church—I really didn't want to come at all. Because it was a choral service, I came. That was the only reason! Then I came back on Easter—twice! And then the next week—twice. And then the next week—twice." On Pentecost, her new church community celebrated God's grace in her life as the waters of baptism confirmed her decision to follow Jesus in the company of four thousand new friends.

On any given Sunday morning, thousands in Chicago will stroll along Lake Michigan; scores in New York City will enjoy an ethnic brunch; armies of bicyclists will ride across the Golden Gate Bridge from San Francisco to Sausalito. In Alexandria, hundreds will catch an extra hour of sleep before heading to the office, while many in Raleigh will rise early for a day trip to the beach, and carloads of Atlantans will tailgate at Turner Field. Though far fewer in number, on every Sunday morning of the year, women and men, children and youth, singles and families, divorced and married, gay and straight, infirm and healthy walk into buildings with the majestic Gothic beauty of the Fourth Presbyterian Church in Chicago or the southern colonial charm of the White Memorial Presbyterian Church in Raleigh or the ornate elegance of the Calvary Presbyterian Church in San Francisco.

Some people come to church today to retreat into an irretrievable and largely imagined past, when life was simpler and truth less complex. Some come to confirm petty moralisms and retreat behind a thin theology. Some come mainly as religious consumers looking for the best deal available currently in what Roof calls the "spiritual marketplace." Some people come, though, to hear words of truth and wrestle with personal and professional enticements to find meaning outside the faith and beyond the church.

Increasingly, individuals come to church because of a desire to be a part of a community of meaning. Roof writes: "Denominationally

based communities can be spiritually supportive for inner circles
and still define boundaries of social interaction that extend well
beyond Sunday morning. They function as a basis for voluntary
organizations and civic activities, less today than in the past, but
more so than secular commentators are inclined to think in a
highly mobile and seemingly rootless world."[9] People come to
church today to find a community of Christian values, to no
longer worship God on their own, but in the company of people
who share common desires and work within a similar ethic. They
come to be forgiven and challenged, to learn the enduring language of faith and to minister to people in need. While the majority of Americans stay home, churchgoers come to commit to a
compelling vision of a corporate life that feeds hungry souls,
quenches spiritual thirst, and advocates for mercy and justice now.
They come to find meaning and to make a meaningful difference,
and to fling doors wide open to any and all who want to follow
Jesus on the kingdom road.

What happens when they arrive? George MacLeod, founder of
the Iona Community, has said: "The trouble with the Church these
days is that no one any longer thinks it is worth persecuting. The
Church is regarded not with hostility, so much as with something
like amused tolerance, or perhaps indifference and apathy."[10]
Norman Shanks, current leader of the Iona Community, expands
MacLeod's thought: "The Church is perceived as of no conse-
quence in relation to the pressing social and political issues of the
day . . . with little help to contribute to the big social and economic questions. And there may also be the notion that . . . commitment to the Church demands the acceptance of a package of
beliefs that are not quite intellectually respectable. For many too
the Church's language and music, its whole ritual and order of
priorities is seen to be rooted in an alien culture. . . . Against this
background, these perceptions and prejudices, what place can the
Church have, whether as provider, as some would have it, of
'social glue,' seeking to hold communities together, or as pointer
to deeper realities for which some may be searching but others
may not wish to acknowledge?"[11] Of the American denominational experience, Roof warns: "Organized religion can be expe-

rienced as distant and out-of-date; spiritually it can be dry. People may, and often do, feel somewhat removed from whatever religious heritage they have inherited."[12]

MacLeod and Shanks speak to the enormous challenge before the church when women and men make the increasingly unpopular and uncommon choice to come to church. What then keeps people coming? What factors lead them to commit to an organization that much of society considers ill-informed, arcane, stiff, and hypocritical? Why do they decide to enter old church doors when society urges that they walk through so many other bright and shining doors of opportunity? In chapter 2 we will hear their answers, which reveal why people who come to church tend to stay.

Chapter 2

Why They Stay

David Steward, Professor of Religious Education at the Pacific School of Religion, offers a sobering analysis of congregational life in America today: "The whole world is changing, and the church with it. The church should be a quiet place in the storm—a place for renewal and a launching pad. But we find the church itself, and its people, uncertain. Congregational life too frequently alienates rather than supports. It seeks to compete with other institutions in society, and finds itself on the losing end."[13] However, people do come and then stay in congregations today. They make a deliberate choice from a myriad of other legitimate and alluring claims on their time, energy, and resources. Why?

In the American religious past, the most obvious reason people came to church and then stayed was family. Typically, as adults, people sought out a congregation within the denomination in which they were born and raised. North American theologian Douglas John Hall explains: "The Christendom into which I was born . . . no longer exists—pockets and vestiges of it notwithstanding. Few people in the Western world today are 'caused' to be Christians by the sheer accident of birth. Many may start out that way, but fewer and fewer find inherited Christianity reason enough to stay Christian."[14] As a case in point, the majority of new members joining the six Presbyterian congregations in this study come from other than a Presbyterian background,[15] and the congregation's Presbyterian identity is rarely a clearly stated reason for why they come or stay.

The third question in each group interview asked participants to identify two or three of the essential emphases of the Reformed/Presbyterian tradition. Respondents who were least acquainted with the Reformed/Presbyterian tradition made these and similar comments:

> To be honest, I don't know what distinguishes a Presbyterian from a Methodist. And I couldn't tell you how a Methodist differs from a Baptist.

> It didn't matter to me what the shingle on the door was. I was raised Methodist and I used to live a half a block away from this church, so I stumbled in one day and it was like, "Oh, my God, I've found it!" If I moved, I'd be looking more for the community, not so much what the brand of the church is.

> I'm not sure that it matters a whole lot to me. If I were to move to another city, I would be looking for another congregation like this one, not necessarily for a Presbyterian church.

> I've always believed that Presbyterians, Methodists, Lutherans, basically believed the same things. But I'm not really sure what Presbyterians believe in that others do not.

Midway through each group interview, the participants were asked: Would you be an active member of this particular congregation were it not a Presbyterian church? Lifelong Presbyterians in every city most often said no, while lifelong Christians who are now Presbyterians, and new Christians, most often said yes. There are still some people, principally lifelong Presbyterians, who deliberately come to and then join a congregation because of its denominational label, but that number is dwindling.

And yet large numbers of people are coming to the six Presbyterian congregations that participated in the study. Not only are people coming, but they are staying. They are making professions of faith and being baptized or reaffirming their faith. They are leading committees, singing in choirs, teaching Sunday school, assisting in worship, serving as ordained and installed elders and deacons, and significantly shaping the institutional life of these Presbyterian congregations. If a high percentage of those coming to church today are not searching for the Presbyterian "brand" of the Christian faith, then why do they remain in a Presbyterian congregation?

Some people stay in Presbyterian congregations because of the appeal of its form of church government. Presbyterianism takes its name from the Greek word *presbuteros,* "elder," and means a government by elected and ordained elders. Laine, a new Christian living in Alexandria, said: "The government aspect of Presbyterianism is really important to me. There's no one sitting there forcing you to go to a congregational meeting and vote aye or nay. But the option is there for you and that just doesn't happen in a lot of places and, personally, that's important to me." Morgan, a new member of her congregation in San Francisco, observed: "It's much more democratic than the other churches to which I've belonged. There really seems to be a tendency to get everybody involved in all kinds of facets of outreach and in church management."

In particular, many churchgoers are drawn to the connectional and representative qualities of Presbyterian polity. Steve, a new Christian from Chicago, said: "I find an unexplainable comfort in knowing that all Presbyterian congregations are connected somehow"; while Marguerite, in San Francisco, argued: "There's a great strength in the Presbyterian willingness to grapple collectively with decisions." Respondents both laughed and moaned about the Presbyterian proclivity to rule by committee. Even so, they appreciated church government that does not bombard them with dictates from on high, nor dissolve into an unruly pure democracy. They especially value a polity in which clergy and laity rule together and with equal voice.

The intellectual challenges and educational emphases in the Reformed/Presbyterian tradition are part of the reason why many members stay in Presbyterian congregations. Sometimes chided for a lack of emotional fervor, Presbyterians have long followed the tutelage of their Genevan mentor, John Calvin, stressing "the life of the mind in the service to God." Madison, a lifetime member of his Presbyterian congregation in Raleigh, confessed: "One thing that appeals to me about the Presbyterian Church is that I need a place where my faith can grow and be stretched, and it can here." In Atlanta, Dina, a newly baptized young Presbyterian, commented: "One thing I like about the Presbyterian church is the sermons, the intellectual side of it, the aspect of reason and intellect and the celebration of reason, rather than just emotion." Sheila and Johannes, two relatively new members of their congregation in Raleigh, added:

Presbyterians place a great emphasis on ongoing education and thinking for yourself rather than being told what you must believe.

We are expected to do some thinking for ourselves and I like that. And if we don't all agree, that's okay.

People come to church today expecting congregations not to underestimate their intelligence, but instead to make them think critically about what it means to be a person to whom God has given both faith and reason. They then appreciate the value of an educated clergy and an educated laity. People stay in congregations in which they are not expected to digest ancient dogma or to recite historic creeds without adequate explanation and interpretation, but, instead, are encouraged to probe and to explore.

Wade Clark Roof argues that the religious experience of many churchgoers today is characterized by "questing." He writes: "The current religious situation in the United States is characterized not so much by a loss of faith as a qualitative shift from unquestioned belief to a more open, questing mood . . . a search for certainty, but also the hope for a more authentic, intrinsically satisfying life."[16] Older adults, baby boomers, and many young persons on the edge of faith stay in congregations in which the Bible is neither proclaimed literally nor discarded as a useless museum piece, but is taught with critical care so members can hear anew the good news of the gospel.[17] Any congregation that does not provide its membership multiple opportunities to hone both their faith and reason will soon find its worship and mission stagnant.

Scripture takes precedence over tradition in Reformed theology, and active church members today value the seriousness and acuity with which their congregation approaches biblical studies.

Joshua, a member new to the Presbyterian church in Raleigh, stressed: "There's an openness in Presbyterianism to different biblical interpretations, which is very important to me coming from an evangelical background that was quite rigid." In San Francisco, Ashley and Ben, lifelong Christians who are also new to the Presbyterian Church, reflected:

> Something that has struck me about Presbyterian churches is the emphasis on the spirit of the law versus the letter of the law in both governing issues and even in the interpretation of the Bible.

> Presbyterians do not use the Bible to beat you over the head!

The above comments do not accurately reflect the current chasm between some believers about responsible ways to read and interpret scripture within the Presbyterian Church (U.S.A.). They do reflect the gratitude frequently expressed by respondents for the freedom of biblical inquiry and respect for those who reach differing conclusions in the Reformed/Presbyterian tradition. Priscilla, who has belonged to several Presbyterian congregations across the nation, offered a hopeful word amid the fierce biblical controversies currently raging within the Presbyterian Church (U.S.A.). She said: "We don't always believe the same thing about the Bible, but we do a pretty decent job of getting along." One can only pray that this member's local experience might find a comparable expression at the national level of every mainline denomination.

Some members join a Presbyterian congregation because they resonate with the particular emphases of Reformed theology. A major theological emphasis in Reformed theology is the sovereignty of God. Arnold, a lifelong Presbyterian from Chicago, expressed it well: "In our theology, we point to God as the Sovereign One and remind ourselves that God picks us. God is the One who starts the stuff." Members new to the Presbyterian Church rejoiced that guilt was rarely used by leaders in their congregation to urge members to attend and to believe in certain prescribed ways. Ernest, a New Yorker now living in San Francisco, observed:

"The Presbyterian church allows you to approach the Christian faith from a lot of different perspectives and in a nonjudgmental fashion." Throughout the study, though unaware, church members emphasized such prominent Reformed theological emphases as the grace of God, the forgiveness of sins, the centrality of worship, the importance of the preached Word, the expectation to lead an ethical and humble life, and a commitment to ecumenism.

Especially attractive to many church members is the commitment in the Reformed/Presbyterian tradition to bring God's word of mercy and love to bear in the public arena. Ellen, in Atlanta, joined Central Presbyterian Church because it is "the church that stayed," the title of a book about this congregation's longstanding decision to be a telling presence of the love of Christ in downtown Atlanta. Ellen offered this praise of another woman in her congregation: "This person really does accept that the face of Christ is on everyone she meets. She actively works for the kingdom of God to break through in this world, but she doesn't see it as something that she's going to make happen. And somehow all of this gives her a serenity that is not naive and a fearlessness to go ahead." Chen Lee, a teacher in his Presbyterian congregation in San Francisco, remarked: "For me, Presbyterianism is a good way to live in the community and worship in faith." Abby, a member of Fifth Avenue Presbyterian Church in New York City, applauded the emphasis on responsible citizenship in Reformed theology. She said: "It [the Presbyterian Church] has a heritage of being involved in the public arena and encouraging members to be responsible citizens."[18]

Many church members in the study could not articulate what makes the Reformed/Presbyterian tradition distinctive within the Christian family. Moreover, they would often disparage denominational identity as a meaningless religious artifact, and thus dismiss it as a contributing factor to their church involvement. Ironically, then, without realizing it, they would cite the unique qualities of Presbyterian polity, theology, worship, and social engagement as significant reasons for why they stay.

Beyond theological and denominational traditions, the most common reason people stay in church today is "the people," those daily living examples of the Christian faith in action. In one of his earliest letters, the apostle Paul charges the Thessalonians to put their Christian faith into practice: "We urge you, beloved, to admonish the idlers, encourage the fainthearted, help the weak, be patient with all of them. See that none of you repays evil for evil, but always seek to do good to one another and to all. Rejoice always, pray without ceasing, give thanks in all circumstances . . . hold fast to what is good; abstain from every form of evil" (1 Thess. 5:14–22 NRSV).

People stay in church today when they see something of Paul's charge to the Thessalonians put into practice, individually and corporately. Anne, in Alexandria, commented on a member of her congregation: "He's very busy, has a whole lot going on in his life, but he has a balance." Sung Tae, recently baptized in Raleigh, was impressed by many members of his new congregation: "They have an obvious spiritual dimension; you have the feeling that they are comfortable and confident in their relationship with God." James, a member of the same congregation, praised another member with these words: "Her faith simply glows in everything she does. She makes me feel positive about my own faith because hers is so strong." Harriet, in Chicago, admired the faith of one member because: "Her spirit and her Christian walk are very evident, not only in her words but in what she does." People who come to church today stay when they meet pastors, lay leaders, and members whose faith runs deep and whose Christian example is obvious.

People are attracted to congregations in which they find good listeners. Herb, a lay leader in his congregation in Alexandria, respected another member because: "She is someone you can go to in a bind. She is reliable, thoughtful, and somebody you can talk to." Active church members across the nation praise those special members with a capacity and willingness to listen. Brian, a new Christian in San Francisco, paid this compliment to another member of his congregation: "He's a good listener and he's able to make you feel special—like you're the only person in the world that matters when you are talking to him." People stay in congregations that extend the gift of listening through structured programs like Stephen Ministry, as well as by the commitment to careful listening by individual members.

A familiar psalm of thanksgiving begins: "Make a joyful noise to the LORD, all the earth. Worship the LORD with gladness; come into his presence with singing" (Ps. 100:1–2 NRSV). In a frequently joyless society and in a workplace that often takes itself too seriously, those coming to church today often stay when they find people with an abiding joy and gladness and the ability to laugh at themselves. Commenting on several members of her congregation in Raleigh, Kate observed: "They have so much joy in what they do. Not only through their humor, but they are just genuinely glad. They do things not for notoriety or fame, but because they get a pleasure themselves, which is contagious. It's a pleasure to be around them." Nick, in Chicago, reflected on qualities of another member: "She is able to laugh and brings out the best in everyone she meets."

In addition to a perceived balance, joy, and willingness to listen, people stay in congregations in which they see members make tough faith-based decisions. Ed and Jackie, two members of a congregation in Atlanta, applauded certain members of their congregation:

He made a significant change in his career to defend the underprivileged from his faith standpoint. I have enormous respect for anybody who makes that kind of commitment.

They've been lifetime members here, and they're elderly now. It would be so easy for them to say, "I can't do this now." But every Sunday, they're just going strong and it's amazing to me.

Charlie, in San Francisco, heaped comparable praise on another member of his congregation: "He demonstrates a life of candor, love and genuine friendship to anyone, regardless of their social or economic position in life. He is outspoken about what is right." An active young professional in Chicago, heavily involved in his congregation's AIDS ministry, said: "As a gay man, it's really important to have someplace like this where I can feel safe and also where I can take comfort that the church is paying attention to what is going on around us in the world." People stay in congregations in which the Christian faith factors heavily into the decisions members make and in which people find a safe and supportive place to live out their faith.

An especially important reason why people stay in congregations today is that they are encouraged to explore their own faith—often for the first time. Randy, a lay leader in his congregation in San Francisco, argued: "An essential of the Christian faith is that you have to be prepared to grow. To be Christian is to accept that you're not perfect and you're going to learn new things and God is going to push you in new directions and you have to be willing to go there." Greg, in Atlanta, described the change of perspective brought about by his Christian life: "Christianity has a way of looking at things that I have never thought about." Maryann, a member of the same congregation, said: "Christianity is counter-cultural. I look at what we see in newspapers and on the news and see that our culture places a high value on having the right place to live, the right car to drive, and on and on. Then I come here and realize that all I have and all I need comes from God. I need to come here to worship that God." Healthy and faithful congregations foster realistic expectations. Douglas John Hall speaks for every church in every age of whatever denomination when he writes: "There is no such thing as a 'perfect' church, and the people who go about looking for such an ideal are bound to be disappointed. The Christian gospel isn't about the perfect church, it's about the perfect love of God, which none of us deserves, and from which we all fall short."[19] Church leaders and members who know and acknowledge the foibles and shortcomings of their congregation model a dependence on God's forgiveness and grace upon which every Christian relies.

At the close of a lengthy and intricate theological argument, Paul charges the Christians in Rome: "Welcome one another, therefore, just as Christ has welcomed you, for the glory of God" (Rom. 15:7 NRSV). A major motivator to stay in a congregation today is the welcome people receive initially and the welcome they continue to experience. Listen to a nationwide chorus of voices commend the welcoming spirit of members in their congregations:

"He has a welcoming spirit. He is gracious, inclusive of other people, goes out of his way to make other people feel welcome, especially new people," said Lonnie, a new member of his congregation in Raleigh.

"This person took an extra moment just to talk to me and make me feel welcome," said Justine, a new Christian living in Atlanta.

"She's genuinely friendly, has a positive attitude, and always makes people feel welcome," said Jeff, a lifetime member of his congregation in Chicago.

"She totally took us under her wing and introduced us to people and got us involved in different activities. I think that a big part of getting people to join the church is making people feel really comfortable before they even join," said Alice and Al, relatively new members of their congregation in Alexandria.

Impressed by the welcoming spirit of an ordained elder in the San Francisco congregation, Mary commented: "He knew everything about everyone who was joining. And then he doesn't forget about them or abandon them."

In a rapidly changing society that emphasizes speed and mobility, which can easily result in a sense of anonymity and isolation, people who venture into Christian congregations today stay because in church they are known by something other, and far more significant, than their job or social security number or Internet password.[20]

Along with receiving a warm and genuine welcome, people stay in congregations in which they can form significant relationships. People prize relationships with other Christians, with whom they can share the joys and agonies of faith's discoveries.[21] In New York, Sal used these words to commend another member: "You can always go to him in a bind, he is always there when something happens, has the ability to make you feel special, is reliable and thoughtful and somebody you can talk to about anything." In an increasingly depersonalized society, people value congregations in which they are allowed the chance to carve out deep and abiding relationships with people who know them by name and offer them a receptive environment in which to share any question or worry or joy. Therefore, David Steward concludes: "Congregations need to listen to people in order to acknowledge the gifts God has given through them and to glorify God for these blessings."[22] People join congregations of every size because they find there people and leaders who know them, welcome and listen to them, take them seriously, and love them.

Delivering his Sermon on the Mount, Jesus warns all those listening to him against parading one's faith for public acclaim: "Whenever you give alms, do not sound a trumpet before you, as the hypocrites do in the synagogues and in the streets, so that they may be praised by others" (Matt. 6:2 NRSV). Against the backdrop of a culture that urges self-promotion and loves the sound of a blaring trumpet, some stay in congregations because it is there they meet men and women of genuine humility and quiet giving. Kati, in Raleigh, admired the humble service of another member of her congregation: "I appreciate her quiet service, no big splash, no sign saying: 'Look at me!' She does what she does behind the scenes." Wayne, a member of the same congregation, praised the Christian life of another member: "He's always doing something for other people, and yet a lot of people do not know about it. He goes about it very quietly." In Atlanta, Gail was moved by the selfless act of another longtime member: "He brings contributions anonymously to the outreach center every Friday, and I believe I'm the only person who knows he does this." People stay in congregations in which they see authentic, non-ostentatious examples of commitment, sacrifice, and generosity by leaders and members.

In a fractious and often contentious time in Christian denominations and congregations, many people are drawn to pastors and members who strive to keep an open mind toward diverse expressions of the faith, new ways to worship, and divergent positions on theological and social issues. Leigh, in Atlanta, commented on an admired member: "She maintains a dedication and commitment to the church even when she doesn't always agree with the way things are going." A similar comment was made by Debbie in Chicago: "He cares about the church and its people; he does not always agree with the direction of the church, but he maintains his respect and participation." Ken, a new Christian in New York City, observed: "His faith is a real inspiration to me. He's not necessarily happy about everything that has happened in the church, but he has stayed." People stay in congregations in which differences are honored within an atmosphere of mutual respect.

Douglas John Hall provides an important theological perspective on the value of Christian hospitality and respect. He writes: "The biblical exhortation is not 'Smother others,' but 'Welcome them.' That means, among other things, 'Let them be themselves! Don't try to overcome the distance between you and them by robbing them of their difference.' That difference is the presupposition of your achieving a real relationship with them."[23] One reason congregations grow despite the cultural decline of the church is that they demonstrate and cultivate an atmosphere of mutual respect and regard.

People stay in congregations in which God's power transforms people to engage in acts of Christian love in and outside the church. Critical of expressions of a narcissistic spirituality among Christians today, Robert Wuthnow writes: "It diverts little of their attention. It does not require them to set aside portions of their day to pray, worship, read sacred texts, reflect on ways to deepen their relationship with God, or be of service to others."[24] Diane, a new Christian from Chicago, spoke about an important lesson she had learned from other Christians: "I have learned that Christ is love and that we are known by name and it makes a difference that we're here and that we are given more by God than we can ever give back. But part of our response to God's great love is to give that love back in any way we can." Graham, in Alexandria, made a similar observation: "I appreciate the opportunity to do good in the community, particularly with those in the greatest need. You simply do not have the same access and impetus to help outside the church." Over against a thin diet of narcissistic Christianity, growing congregations challenge members to follow Jesus into the world God so loves.

Novelist John Updike offers this literary flourish on the current state of the Christian church, at least the Protestant version: "A Protestant Christian on the eve of the third millennium must struggle with the sensation that his sect is, like the universe itself, in the latest cosmological news, winding down, growing thinner and thinner."[25] Wade Clark Roof delivers a more sociological assessment of the state of Christendom, particularly Protestantism: "Among mainline Protestants in the United States . . . an erosion of religious commitment is discernible dating from the early decades of this century."[26] Updike and Roof describe what any seasoned church leader or churchgoer already knows: People may initially come to church out of a lingering sense of guilt or habit or family tradition, but with few cultural enforcers any longer in place, these are insufficient reasons for people to stay.

The church of Christ Jesus in America no longer owns exclusive rights to people's attention or allegiance. Some Christians find this a reason to panic, to batten down the hatches, and to try to reclaim an idealized past. Norman Shanks, leader of the Iona Community—a nonresident, religious community, based in Scotland—poses a far richer vision for Christian congregations: "The Church is going to have to overcome the resistance to innovation, exploration and experiment, lay aside the reluctance to take risks, and put behind it the preoccupation with survival. . . . It is a natural tendency in adversity to entrench, to seek to do the old, familiar things even better. But the cause of the kingdom calls for a different direction from this entirely, the essence of the gospel and the loving purposes of God have to do with risk, surprise, the doing of a 'new thing,' and the insight that fullness of life is to be experienced only through being prepared to give it away."[27] Congregations that embrace Shanks's vision do not take for granted that people will come to church today, but instead develop new, creative, and compelling reasons for people to do so.

So when people do make the increasingly less likely choice to come to church today, what are some reasons they stay? They stay because those already there do not treat them as intruders, but welcome and embrace and invite them to walk the road less traveled. They come as individual religious consumers, but they stay because they embrace the empowering character of a corporate identity. In these congregations, they find people who make time to listen and then do so with sensitivity, respect, and care; people who give generously without fanfare and whose manner demonstrates a depth of uncommon joy; people whose lives in and out of the church manifest a faith in Christ; people willing to confront the powerful on behalf of the broken and disenfranchised; and people upon whom one can depend despite profound personal or theological differences. Though often unaware, people who come to church also stay because of the distinctive theology, polity, and worship of the congregation's denomination.

For those who come to church and stay, what then draws them into a weekly service of corporate worship? Every Sunday in America, people stroll to Fourth, take a taxi to Fifth Avenue, battle the beltway to Westminster, take a trolley to Calvary, weave their way to White Memorial, and converge upon Central, along with hundreds and thousands of members in other congregations, to worship God. Why? Why do they join in an activity that many in society today consider a rusty remnant of a former day? In chapter 3 we will explore what compels people into corporate worship two thousand years after the birth of Christ.

Chapter 3

Why They Worship

On a recent Sunday morning, Stewart, an active member of a San Francisco church, left his house dressed in a suit. His neighbor who was outside retrieving the morning paper greeted him. "You heading to work?" asked the neighbor innocently. Where else would someone dressed in a coat and tie be heading on a Sunday morning in America today? This man was not on his way to work, but on his way to worship with other believers—a regular activity for him on almost every Sunday of the year, but an activity increasingly viewed as peripheral or odd, or simply ignored by the larger society.

In a culture that no longer automatically links spiritual growth to a worshiping community[28] and increasingly displays apathy or disdain toward any church, why do well-educated, articulate, urbane, highly skilled people worship today? Worshipers asked in a written questionnaire to estimate their frequency of Sunday morning worship over a three-month period, recorded similar responses with remarkable regularity across the country. Lifelong members of a particular denomination and lifelong Christians who have belonged to more than one denomination were the most frequent worshipers, averaging ten Sundays over a three-month period. New Christians varied in attendance, some averaging eleven Sundays over a three-month period, while other new Christians averaged but six Sundays in the same period. On most Sundays, Christians across the nation still get out of bed, dress, leave for church, and worship with other people who made the same choice. Why?

A common reason people worship is that they experience an ill-defined, but compelling need to do so. They speak of corporate worship not as an addendum to their other church involvement, but as its pivot point. In San Francisco, Louise, a leader in her congregation, said it this way: "I worship because it keeps me grounded in what I believe." Stephanie, a lifetime member of a downtown congregation in Atlanta, observed: "I worship in response to a lifelong intrigue with the question, 'What is our chief end?'" Will, a Chicago churchgoer, confessed: "I have a need for it. There's a hunger inside when I do not worship." Caroline, a member of the same Chicago congregation, added: "It's very important for me to spend one part of one day every week in worship and in appreciation to God." People worship, at least in part, as a natural expression of their God-given identity and purpose.

When people worship, especially in urban settings, they bring with them all the scars of a transitory, anonymous, and frantic society. Typically living far from extended family, frequently single or divorced, with few natural connections to other members of the congregation, the people who sit in pews today often arrive with a profound loneliness and feeling of displacement, and bring with them a yearning to belong to a caring community of believers.[29] They often eat alone, work alone, exercise alone, and many have tried to worship alone and found the experience wanting.[30] Harvey, a new Christian in Chicago, described a common pilgrimage among American worshipers today: "When I was in high school and college, I would say, 'Well, I have my own private spirituality and I can talk to God on my own and I don't really need a church. Where in the Bible does it say you must go to Sunday worship to have a conversation with God?' But for me, what I really gain out of Sunday worship is the sense that there are so many other people here that have similar faith and beliefs as you. You're not alone and there is a sense of community in the truest sense of the word."

People worship today because they experience a personal need and desire to do so, but they bring with them an equally strong need and desire to do so with a comparatively committed community of Christians. Homer, a new Christian in Raleigh, said: "I appreciate the warm feeling I get from gathering with such a large number of other Christians in worship. Though it is very large, it feels like a family." Leomont, a longtime Presbyterian from Atlanta, reflected on why he worships: "The people there are the most meaningful thing to me because they are a body of believers. I mean, I could turn on the radio and listen to preaching. I wouldn't, but I could. Being here in community is what's the most meaningful to me." Nora, another member of the same congregation, had recently returned to church after years away. She said: "I fell away for some years and what brought me back was this feeling that I had to be worshiping with other people. Corporate worship. That's what started me back." Separated from family and typically stressed by work and home environments, people come to worship in congregations in which they can express their faith and have their faith strengthened through the interchange of ideas, service and devotion in a community of committed believers.

People worship in congregations that maintain a vitality and vision for the praise of God and work of Christ rather than dwelling on numbers—either rising or falling. Nile Harper connects vital worship with broad vision and vigorous service: "The most dynamic sign in urban churches is the increasingly vigorous and creative worship taking place in a growing number of city congregations. In many city churches, worship is spiritually powerful, culturally diverse, and directly related to mission. Renewed worship is designed to speak to the mind as well as the heart and soul. People are being educated to act from faith, hope, and love in order to bring compassion, new life, and justice into neighborhoods."[31] The experience of divine worship described in scripture prepares the people of God for a continuous experience of praise, confession, and acts of love in and out of the congregation.

It should come as no surprise to see sanctuaries empty and church doors closed when worship serves as the prop for a declining institution rather than reflecting the invigorating presence of the Spirit of God. As church membership dwindles and worship attendance declines in the postmodern era, clergy, lay leaders, and members often panic and look for people or events to blame. Rather than exploring new avenues for evangelism and mission, some people point fingers at those who look different from or behave in ways outside the congregational norm, by whose very presence and participation, they suggest, the church is compromised or corrupted.

Fearing further loss, congregations and denominations tend to close ranks and exclude these people that society or religious prejudice deems marginal. This is hardly a new phenomenon. Throughout history, the people of God have sometimes felt a need to narrow the borders of the community, meticulously detailing who is in and who is out, publishing some form of purity code to which all who would worship God in that community must adhere.

In Israel, following the Babylonian exile, a battle was waged over an inclusive or exclusive understanding of the nature of God and the composition of God's people. Much of Third Isaiah proclaims a God who includes, while Israel was closing its borders, force-marching aliens from the land, and building gates to cordon off the community from outside pollutants. Old Testament scholar Walter Brueggemann reflects on Third Isaiah and the issue of inclusion or exclusion in conversation with today's church: "Nervous people exclude. In the church . . . exclude homosexuals. In the civil community . . . exclude undocumented workers and other threatening outsiders. Exclude and make it safe for us. Thus after exile, there is in the Jewish community a drive for exclusiveness and purity . . . only Jews, pure Jews, only Jews like us." And then comes Isaiah 56:

> To the eunuchs[32] who keep my sabbaths,
>   who choose the things that please me
>   and hold fast my covenant,
> I will give, in my house and within my walls,
>   a monument and a name
>   better than sons and daughters;
> I will give them an everlasting name
>   that shall not be cut off.
> And the foreigners who join themselves to the LORD
>   to minister to him, to love the name of the LORD,
>   and to be his servants,
> all who keep the sabbath and do not profane it,

> and hold fast my covenant—these I will bring to my holy
> mountain,
> and make them joyful in my house of prayer . . .
> Thus says the LORD GOD,
> who gathers the outcasts of Israel,
> I will gather others to them,
> besides those already gathered. (vv. 4–8 NRSV)

Brueggemann concludes: "The God who gathers intends a community that gathers."[33]

In contrast to current tendencies in mainline denominations to tighten qualifications for membership and leadership, worshipers today tend to value the inclusive tendencies of their particular congregation, in which a rich diversity of believers and would-be believers can gather and be embraced without special qualifications. Sammy, a new Presbyterian in Chicago, echoed a common sentiment of worshipers across America: "It's wonderful worshiping in a place where I belong with people who are remarkably different from me and yet we are all made welcome and included." Douglas John Hall gives theological expression to this move away from exclusivity. He writes: "Far from sanctioning or encouraging the 'natural' habit of exclusion, the grace that comes from that Source constantly judges that habit, and strives to replace it with at least the beginnings of a far greater openness to other—greater, indeed, than I usually find comfortable."[34]

Church members today generally appreciate worshiping with a diversity of people, who bring with them a wide range of faith, experience, and understanding. Fewer churchgoers today want to worship simply with theological, social, political, sexual, or economic mirror images. Instead, they desire to worship with people who are prepared to keep minds and hearts and doors open, especially to people for whom the church has traditionally offered less than an enthusiastic welcome. Congregations that experience sustained growth in membership and worship attendance most often do so because they do not place restrictive obstacles to be overcome before visitors can worship and participate fully in the life of the congregation.

In the twenty-first century, people are less likely to worship in the religious tradition of their immediate family or ancestors.[35] On any given Sunday morning, those greeted on the steps of Calvary Presbyterian in San Francisco or welcomed in the narthex of Fifth Avenue Presbyterian in Manhattan come to Presbyterian worship mainly from other worship traditions—ranging from Quaker to Roman Catholic to Disciples of Christ, with nearly one quarter of those coming to church arriving with no significant worship experience at all. Diversity in their worship background is the rule among those interviewed, with a minority of lifelong adherents to a particular tradition of worship insisting that it remain unchanged.

What then does this liturgically eclectic collection of Christians, now worshiping in Presbyterian congregations, find the most meaningful about the worship experience? Historically reticent to prescribe one order of worship, Presbyterian liturgies vary somewhat from congregation to congregation. However, with the publication of a *Book of Common Worship,* which suggests an order of worship for the Lord's Day and the increased use of the Revised Common Lectionary by Presbyterian pastors, the Sunday morning worship service in most Presbyterian congregations today is quite uniform.[36]

Worshipers today value a well-reasoned and carefully executed worship service. Steven, someone new to the Christian faith and worship in Chicago, marveled: "There seems to be a theme almost every Sunday so that I can remember it after I leave. I guess a lot of that is planned." Karen, a Christian in Alexandria, noted the importance of a liturgy upon which people can rely: "The order of service is important to me. You can expect this and that to happen at certain times." Marcus, an active churchgoer in Atlanta, enjoyed the flexibility within the Presbyterian liturgy: "I appreciate the order and stability, but what I find most meaningful are the worship services when I am surprised. The possibility of a surprise is what I find particularly engaging." Tony, an elder in his congregation in Atlanta, articulated an observation made in different ways in congregations across the country: "I value our liturgy. There's a very significant integrity about the preparation of the service and all the elements from the prelude right through the postlude." Christians today are drawn to a service of worship with a sound theological rationale, a logical liturgical flow, and enough flexibility to allow for occasional variations from the norm, as long as the service maintains a genuine liturgical integrity.

Historically and theologically, Protestant worship, especially within the Presbyterian tradition, has placed considerable emphasis on the preached word. In recent decades, as churches across the denominational spectrum have undergone a liturgical renewal, there has been a tendency in "preaching-centered" liturgies to deemphasize the central focus on the preached word in worship and to elevate the role of other parts of the liturgy. Yet despite these recent liturgical trends in "preaching-centered" traditions, worship planners and leaders would be well served not to underestimate the importance of the sermon to the overall worship experience.

The fifth question asked of participants in the group interview was: "What do you find most meaningful about the worship experience at your congregation?" The initial response of most active churchgoers in the study centered overwhelmingly on the sermon:

> The sermons here are in touch with reality. The message is clear and stays with you. I keep the sermons and read them again and again.

> I'm really drawn here by the sermons. Even though there are so many people in the services, you feel like the pastor is addressing you and makes you feel important that you are there.

> I appreciate the preaching. The sermons get to the point without telling a lot of cute little stories, and the preachers are not afraid to tackle difficult biblical texts and social and political issues.

> For the first time in my life, I really look forward to hearing sermons. They don't underestimate my intelligence and they are relevant.

Administrative, pastoral, teaching, and civic expectations and responsibilities can easily drain a minister's time, creativity and energy in today's church environment. Despite the multiple and varied demands placed upon worship leaders, congregations respect preachers who regularly spend significant time in sermon preparation.

The importance of the sermon to liturgies today is heightened by the growing number of worshipers who have little acquaintance with the Bible and those who question whether worship will offer any meaning to their lives. The preacher today can assume little biblical knowledge in those sitting in the pews, and must somehow make relevant the tenets of a book held with suspect relevance, particularly by those new to Christian worship. At the same time, the preacher cannot live in the land of expository preaching and expect worshipers unaided to make contemporary connections to their lives. Sermons must reflect the hard work of faithful biblical exegesis while maintaining a well-read dialogue with the modern world of art, literature, politics, and culture. Finally, sermons must be delivered in a way to appeal to cognition, but also to delve into the heart of the worshiper's religious sentiments. Reflecting many similar views, Rex, a new Christian from Raleigh, said of his pastor: "It's extraordinary to have a preacher who can take ethereal, difficult concepts and make sense of them so that you feel he is talking to you. That's an important gift to hone."

Clearly, worshipers place a high value on good sermons with compelling delivery, but they also appreciate careful attention to every component in worship, from the prelude to the benediction. Cindy, a lifetime Christian living in Chicago, explained: "I appreciate what is said in the preface of the bulletin—'Let us approach God in silence'—which to me, means to shut up all the stuff in my head and be open to listen to all that will follow." Chuck, a member of the same congregation, then commented: "I happen to like the benediction. I love when he says, 'Hold to the good.' I love that. I think I sometimes come just for the benediction." Jennell, new to her church in Raleigh, emphasized the importance of the public offering of one's financial gifts: "It's a great trust that is engendered during those few minutes in the worship service. It means a lot to me to know that the money I give will be used well and help in ways that I would never even imagine."

Occasions to pray in a liturgy also contribute to why people worship today. Candace, from a congregation in Atlanta, said: "I really enjoy the prayers. We have wonderful liturgists in this church who can really pray and make you think deeply about issues and God's involvement in things that are going on around us." Louis, a lay leader in his congregation in Alexandria, exclaimed: "The pastoral prayers. I love those. They always get me because they are things I'm always reading about daily and then when the whole church is sitting there praying for those things, I think, 'This is so good!' "

The First Letter of John contains this piece of liturgy from the first century of the church: "If we say that we have no sin, we deceive ourselves, and the truth is not in us. If we confess our sins, God who is faithful and just will forgive us our sins and cleanse us from all unrighteousness" (1 John 1:8–9, au. trans.). Set in the context of God's transforming grace and assurance of pardon, liturgists have long echoed these words to introduce a time for personal and corporate confession in worship. People need a time in worship to acknowledge their alienation from God and each other and to confess their resulting brokenness. Walt, a new Christian from Raleigh, gave this fresh look at the ancient rite of public confession: "It's liberating and disarming. At the end of it all, I feel like we're on the same page: we're not perfect. Social status, income, race, whatever, we're all on the same page." For worshipers today, prayer during a service of worship is considered as more than merely a liturgical afterthought or a preface to the sermon. Prayer gives worship meaning and context and gives worshipers a voice in liturgies too often dominated by preachers' voices.

One modern criticism of Christian worship centers around prayer. A considerable number of active worshipers today lament the lack of silence in their morning service of worship, especially the brief time typically allowed for silent prayer. Vince, an elder in his congregation in Atlanta, said: "I find the discipline of a period of silence in worship very meaningful, but I feel that it is often missing or far too limited in our worship services. We don't have enough time for silence, and I believe we are frightened by it." Worshipers often think that their worship leaders, more than the worshipers themselves, are uneasy with allowing much silence in the liturgy. In an increasingly noisy world, where unwelcome and unsolicited sounds invade every waking moment, worship leaders would do well to remember the ancient tale of the prophet Elijah, who encounters God, not in the whirlwind or the earthquake, but in the silence (see 1 Kings 19:12–13 NRSV). Worship leaders would then be well-advised to ask themselves: How can we creatively and authentically incorporate the value of silence in a service that is sometimes too noisy?

Even when new to Christian worship or to the liturgical nuances of a different denomination, worshipers quickly grasp the critical role that music plays in Christian worship. Willie, a new Christian from Raleigh, shared a sentiment frequently mentioned: "I find the music extremely meaningful; the blending of the meaning of the text with the emotion of the music takes worship to new levels." Tim and Sarah, two lifetime churchgoers from Chicago, testified to the critical value of hymnody in their appreciation of worship:

I always find the hymn singing to be meaningful. It's such an important part of worship just to have everyone standing together singing.

I like to sit up front and listen to the voices singing when the church is full.

People appreciate the way that good hymnody teaches the biblical story, explicates a sound theology, and unites a diverse body of people, even though there is hardly a consensus among worshipers today about what constitutes "good hymnody."

Despite its agreed-upon importance to worship, music also provokes the widest range of opinions and reveals the deepest chasm between generations and between longer term and newer members. Lanny, a young person, new to the Christian faith in San Francisco, who otherwise was extremely enthusiastic about his worship and church life, leveled this criticism at the Sunday morning service: "The music is so slow and funereal in a lot of the hymns that are chosen. It's almost like the hymns that have a fast tempo are slowed down." Carole, another new Christian from the same church, speculated about why worship leaders in Presbyterian churches select certain hymns: "It seems as though Presbyterian theology prefers the first person plural/Thou relationship in hymns. For me, though, the hymns that instill joy are the I/Thou hymns, which we almost never sing." Mark, another new Christian from the east coast, made a counterpoint: "We all have our preferences when it comes to music, and I enjoy the classically-based repertoire of the choir. It was something that drew me to this church. It was something that was very different from any church I've ever visited."

To avoid making music "the war department of the church," worship leaders need to listen carefully to their members both to discern their musical preferences and to assess their knowledge of the role of music in Christian worship. Thomas Troeger, Professor of Preaching and Communications at the Iliff School of Theology in Denver, Colorado, sounds an important warning and reminder that music in worship must not be restricted to the qualified few. He writes: "Congregational singing is a witness to our belief that worship is based not on the adequacy of our efforts, but on the saving, gracious character of the One we praise. God who forgives sins certainly forgives wrong notes! As singing gives embodied witness to the doctrine of creation, it also gives embodied witness to the doctrine of salvation. Our music is a sign that the saving grace of Christ is freeing us to do what we were created to do—to give ourselves with complete abandonment to God."[37] Worship leaders and church musicians in particular need to engage in ongoing conversations with churchgoers and continue their education about church music so that the church's music is not reserved for a professional elite, but belongs heart and soul to the people of God.

To address the broad scope of opinions about church music and recognizing that worshipers frequently move from one liturgical tradition to another—each having its own appreciation of and approach to church music—a growing number of congregations are offering an alternative or contemporary or blended service of worship. By offering a worship service at a time other than Sunday morning, congregations open church doors to a growing number of people whose work precludes them from participating regularly at the traditional Protestant 11 A.M. worship hour. Warren, a relatively new member of his congregation in San Francisco, expressed a sentiment held by many worship leaders: "This church takes the way the service is put together very seriously and we don't casually change." Even so, this historic congregation has recently added an additional evening worship service. Once a month, this congregation designs a service to address the pain and alienation in its city, nation, and world. Craig, a member of the same congregation, spoke about this service: "My favorite service is the Service of Healing and Wholeness that we have one night a month. The laying on of hands, the communion and the singing. It's the most moving for me of all the services."

Supplemental worship services often incorporate new hymnody, use instruments other than the organ, and include nonclassical music as well as music from the world church, especially from such international worship centers as the Taizé and Iona communities. Scottish hymnwriter John Bell contends: "The church always needs new songs, not because the gospel changes, but because the world changes, and God's purposes in the world have to be reinterpreted to become real for the times. We live in a country where unemployment plagues and demoralizes large sections of our community, and where lochs play host to a nuclear arsenal, but where are the songs of protest? Where are the spiritual songs . . . of a glorious heritage of folk music, of fiddle and pipe tunes, of vocal melodies all in danger of disappearing into oblivion? Where are the words and music which might yet allow those on the fringes of the church, or those who have rejected the trappings of organized religion, to deepen their faith and praise their maker."[38] Given the diversity of liturgical backgrounds and personal needs, there is a growing need among mainline congregations both to enrich traditional worship and to develop new hymnody and new worship practices by creating alternative services of worship, many of which are rooted in ancient Christian liturgical traditions.

The majority of Protestant churches celebrate two sacraments: the Lord's Supper and baptism. Aside from sermons, the sacraments are typically cited by worshipers as most meaningful to their worship experience. This emphasis reflects both a major change in worship practices among most mainline Protestants and a significant shift in perception of those who have worshiped in Protestant communions over the last two or three decades.

As a child raised in the southern tradition of the Presbyterian Church, I rarely witnessed an adult baptism, but within the first few months of 1999 alone, I celebrated the baptism of six adults in the congregation I serve. Increasingly, Protestant congregations, especially in urban areas, are experiencing a noticeable rise in adult baptisms. Taken in its larger religious and sociological context, this phenomenon is hardly surprising. As more people come to church for the first time, especially the children and grandchildren of the non-churchgoing baby boomers, congregations will most likely celebrate the faith-affirming baptism of adult believers with greater frequency.

The majority of worshipers today bring with them an array of religious experiences, as well as diverse perceptions and understandings of the meaning and practice of baptism—everything from nonsacramental Christian Scientists to the believer's baptism tradition of Southern Baptists. In those Protestant traditions that practice infant baptism, people are accustomed to the covenantal nature of the sacrament and the resulting responsibility of the worshiping community toward the child baptized and his or her family. This covenantal emphasis is also expressed when youth and adults are baptized, as a way of reinforcing the building of community associated with baptism.

At the Central Presbyterian Church in Atlanta, during the baptism of an infant, both adults and children in worship are asked to nurture the infant being baptized. A member of that congregation observed: "I appreciate the responsibility this church takes toward its children. As a child, I was always sent off to Junior Church. I was never allowed in the 'big house' with the adults. That is the part of baptism that is so special to me—that those children are asked to accept this infant as their brother or sister. The question

itself helps to empower the children to rise to the occasion."
Another member of the same congregation affirmed the covenantal theme present in the celebration of the sacrament of baptism:
"It brings a tear to my eye when we ask the congregation to help
nurture the child being baptized in her growth as a Christian. We
acknowledge that we are all part of a family, that we are going to
watch out for each other and work together as a team to really
help our children. I don't mean just my own children, but everybody's children." We feel a collective responsibility to instill certain values in our children by allowing them to explore the
Christian faith for themselves in a safe and nurturing environment. In the celebration of baptism, the congregation reminds
itself that the God who enters into a covenant with God's people
also expects God's people faithfully to enter into and honor that
covenant of grace.

A commonly maligned baptismal practice in liturgies today
occurs when the celebrant walks down the aisle to introduce the
child to the congregation that has just committed to his or her
care. This practice is critiqued in certain corners of the church as
leading to an overemphasis on ceremony and a resulting deemphasis on the sacrament. While this criticism needs to be taken
seriously, voices to the contrary need also to be heard. Donald, a
new Christian who is a member of a Raleigh congregation,
reflected: "When they baptize children, they walk the child up and
down the aisle and introduce them to the congregation. It reinforces the idea that this is a community and we're going to support them in their faith. Baptism here is not a private privilege but
it's more of a bringing together of God's people." Worship leaders need to recognize the community building potential within the
sacrament of baptism. They also would do well not to underestimate the important pedagogical possibilities present for families and congregations when the waters of baptism flow for young
or old.

The Lord's Supper is the other sacrament celebrated within
most Protestant traditions. When I was a child, my tradition celebrated the Lord's Supper quarterly, lest it lose its mystery and
meaning by being observed too frequently. Several weeks of

preparation preceded each celebration so that worshipers would not receive the sacrament in an unworthy fashion.[39] The preparation, as the sacrament itself, was intended for adult believers. Members were encouraged to observe an extended period of self-reflection and penance before receiving the holy elements.

As the landscape of worship has changed throughout the Protestant church over the past three decades, so have attitudes toward this sacrament. Denominations and congregations celebrate the sacrament on a variety of liturgical and nonliturgical schedules, but almost every Protestant church celebrates the Lord's Supper with greater frequency than in America's religious past. In the written questionnaire, more than 80 percent of the respondents expressed a strong desire that the sacrament be celebrated with greater frequency than currently practiced in their congregation, with a significant number of them indicating a preference for a weekly celebration.

Why do worshipers commonly call for a greater frequency of celebration? Louie, new to Christian worship and living in San Francisco, commented on the community building value of this sacrament: "I came to this church soon after arriving in town four years ago. Last week, I was giving out the elements on the lectern side and I knew probably 80 percent of the people who came down the aisle and could call them by name. I was quivering when it was all over." Megan, an ordained elder from the same church, professed: "I'd say that the most spiritual thing I've ever done is when I gave the sacrament for the first time." Four and a half centuries ago in Geneva, Switzerland, John Calvin advocated a weekly celebration of this sacrament. Congregations in worship traditions that celebrate the Eucharist infrequently should listen to the voices of members, who sometimes appreciate the spiritual, community building, and pedagogical value of regular celebration of the Lord's Supper more than worship leaders themselves.

Look out over many congregations in worship today and you will see many puzzled faces. As more people step into Christian sanctuaries with no prior worship experience, denominations construct formidable walls unless they make participation in the liturgy intelligible and accessible. As the corporate worship of

God becomes an increasingly countercultural activity in American society, churches must make every effort to decode the language of praise. Worshipers who do not know when to sit or stand, which book to use, the words to a creed or why they are being asked to repeat it, will soon get the message that they do not belong, and often will quietly leave. If worship is to be anything more than an occasional private religious moment, congregations must insure that their public worship offers an unhindered and intelligible opportunity to praise God.

People worship today as an intentional choice that many of their colleagues, neighbors, friends and other family members do not make. They do not necessarily come to worship with a lifetime tradition of worship experience or from a background of family worship practices or with full biblical, theological, or liturgical vocabularies or an awareness of the fine points of church music and worship etiquette. Increasingly, people come to worship not altogether clear about what led them to do so or what to expect. But they come. And, when they do, they expect a worship service which proclaims the holiness of God and also includes them and encourages them to grow in their faith and practice. They expect to be welcomed with open arms into a community of fellow sojourners on the kingdom road. Finally, they expect worship to create an environment to encounter the holy, enriched by the diverse composition of contemporary congregations.[40]

As more people join Christian congregations across denominational traditions and with little religious background at all, they present new possibilities and real challenges for the church. In chapter 4 we will explore the beliefs of those who come to church, decide to stay, and regularly worship; beliefs about the Bible, theology, and about their particular denominational tradition.

What They Believe

Whether a lifetime church member or a fledgling worshiper on the edge of faith,[41] what do churchgoers today believe to be true about Christianity? The second question in the study sought to explore contemporary answers from those now active in congregations. It asked: "Someone from a non-Christian background, whom you know and trust, asks you in all sincerity: 'Can you tell me two or three of the essentials of Christianity, of being Christian?' How would you respond?" In this chapter we will listen to how a nationwide sample of Christians responds to this question and to the question that immediately followed. Their responses reveal a depth of character and an often burgeoning faith, but also some major pedagogical challenges before the church today.

Among current churchgoers in America, Christianity falls into several practical categories. Many describe their Christian faith as a "work in progress," a way of living that, in time, may or may not answer profound theological questions, but will provide a firm foundation for life's journey. Sharon, a member of a congregation in Atlanta, said: "I'm always struck by the fact that Jesus said, 'Follow me,' not 'Do you believe?' It is in the following that we really get to know the Lord." Similarly, Hui, a new Christian from San Francisco, explained: "I view the relationship with God as a journey, becoming closer and closer each day." In Raleigh, Dmitri, also a new Christian, commented: "It's like an endless journey to me. I wouldn't want anyone to feel put off if they did not have all the answers. Christianity is not about having all the answers, but following the One who does." Those who describe the Christian faith as a lifelong journey for meaning also express appreciation for the multiple and diverse ways their local congregations provide direction and wise counsel for their evolving faith.

Another practical category in which people view Christianity today is its sense of community.[42] Churchgoers recognize that Christianity involves major personal decisions, but that the Christian faith is hardly a private religious undertaking. Juan, a lay leader in his congregation in Alexandria, offered a humorous look at this corporate-private dichotomy: "Christians generally like to be together. We don't stay at home and light our candles on our own." Nancy, a member of the same congregation and a recent convert to the Christian faith, spoke these words through tears of joy and appreciation: "I'm a Christian because I belong to a community that's for keeps. If your chips are down or you're sick or if you are helping someone else in those conditions, it's a community for keeps." In these and similar comments, participants reinforced Paul's insight about the communal nature of Christianity: "If one member suffers, all suffer together with it; if one member is honored, all rejoice together with it" (1 Cor. 12:26 NRSV).

The philosophy of self-help groups is another common category used to characterize the Christian faith. Mel, a lifetime Christian from Chicago, said: "Christianity causes you to place less emphasis on yourself and put your ultimate trust in a Higher Power." In San Francisco, Rachel, another lifetime Christian, commented: "Christianity involves a sense of surrender, of letting go of control, and a kind of jumping off and flying." Carol, a new Christian from Atlanta, coined several unique expressions to render a similar sentiment: "Christianity involves a surrender, a willingness to not be in charge and to recognize that this is not just your gig. That's a big relief, but it's also very hard, especially for young, urban Americans to say, 'It's not all up to me.'" Luke, another new Christian from Raleigh, summed it up: "Christianity is giving over your sense of control to God." Such comments suggest that Christians are learning many tenets of the faith today from such para-religious and para-church organizations as

Alcoholics Anonymous. Perhaps the time is ripe for congregations and the Twelve-Step programs that often meet in their basements to deepen their bonds and learn from each other.

Frequently, church members depict the Christian faith as a "leap of faith," a commitment that takes them beyond the borders of proof and reason. Tim, a lifelong Christian from San Francisco, said: "To be Christian is to want God in your life and to accept God's grace and love. That is a giant leap for some folks, and I think we have to tell them there's a wonderful world on the other side of it, but you do first have to make that leap." Kathryn, a member of a congregation in the heart of Manhattan, explained it this way: "Being a Christian requires taking a leap of faith as you acknowledge that there's something bigger and greater in life than what you can understand or fathom. It's having faith in something greater than you." Jack, in Alexandria, gave an answer born of years of sometimes painful experience: "It means to have a deep, deep enduring faith in God. If your faith is deep enough, you can ride through anything that life throws your way."

Some describe essential Christian beliefs by citing broad theological concepts or paraphrasing traditional creedal formulas. Some of the most typical of these responses follow:

> Christians believe in a loving Creator who created us all in His image and who loves us beyond measure and who sent His Son, Jesus, to die for us. And that through Jesus we have forgiveness and we have the opportunity to live, to be in right relationship with God and to live an eternal life.

> Christians believe in forgiveness and grace. They believe that no matter what they do and how much they stumble, Christ died for them and God will forgive them and asks that they practice the same forgiveness with each other.

> I have learned that Christ is love and that we are known by name and it makes a difference that we believe. It means that we have been given more than we can ever give back and that part of Christ's love is to give back in as many ways as we can.

Todd, a new Christian from Atlanta, disputed the notion that Christianity is primarily about right beliefs. He argued for the importance of understanding one's own Christian identity: "To be a good Christian calls for a real sense of curiosity about who we are, what we are, why we are what we are, what is our calling, our reason for being, and trying to take the time to reflect on that and to come to grips and to understand yourself."

"Faith in action" is another category commonly used to describe the Christian faith. Sally, a lifetime member of her congregation in Raleigh, explained: "Christians have an empathy for all people. A Christian is someone who, deep inside, does good things, often when nobody knows about it. And they don't do it for glory or recognition." Mike, an educator from Chicago, said: "Christians try to live by Christ's example, which means to have the courage to do the right thing regardless of the conventional wisdom or the consequences." Emphasizing that Christianity is not a religion of self-absorption, Doug, another member of the same congregation, contended: "Christianity is a quick concern for others. It is a love extended to social outcasts. It isn't about loving other people like you and with whom you feel comfortable."

Christianity described as "faith in action" occurs even more frequently in the written questionnaires. Participants were asked to complete this sentence: "I feel most like a disciple of Jesus when . . ." Over two-thirds of the respondents define Christian discipleship in terms of caring actions motivated by faith in Christ. Answers include: listening to people in need, being a good neighbor, spouse, friend, serving on a church work project, volunteering at an AIDS clinic, serving as a Stephen Minister, protesting against the death penalty, and helping others without expectation of thanks or reward. Most respondents stress that Christian discipleship necessarily involves a life of deliberate compassion and selfless acts of mercy.

A few churchgoers see active and intentional evangelism as an essential part of Christianity. This opinion is expressed most often by new Christians. Sarah, a new Christian from New York, wrote: "When I hear someone witness for Christ, I find myself joyfully saying, 'Amen.' This is probably because I know I was not in a place to understand that twenty or even ten years ago—'I was blind but now I see.'" In Raleigh, Bessie, also a new Christian, wrote: "I feel most like a disciple of Jesus when I can share my faith with others and tell others the joy that comes with faith in Christ." Both in written questionnaires and in oral interviews, new Christians are the most likely to talk freely and enthusiastically about the importance of witnessing to their faith in Christ. These respondents articulate an argument similar to that of Paul in his letter to Rome: "How are they to call on one in whom they have not believed? And how are they to believe in one of whom they have never heard? And how are they to hear without someone to proclaim him?" (Rom. 10:14 NRSV).

Another frequent depiction of the essence of Christianity is that of "quiet faithfulness." Billy, a lay leader in his congregation in Alexandria, wrote: "I feel most like a disciple when I encounter someone whose words or actions are harsh and impatient and I behave in a loving manner toward that person." Donna, another new Christian in Alexandria, described Christianity as "a life of faithful discipleship as when I am able to see the good in people around me and accept their faults as easily as the eighteen-month-olds that I teach in nursery school." Respondents nationwide often refer to the Christian camp song "They Will Know We Are Christians by Our Love" as an ideal depiction of Christian discipleship.

Despite sincere and often remarkable testimonies to their Christian faith and discipleship, church members and lay leaders today possess a limited facility with biblical and theological language. Respondents in the study rarely used or alluded to biblical stories, characters, images, metaphors or similes when they were asked to describe Christian faith and discipleship. In the questionnaires, more than 80 percent of the study's participants indicate that they read the Bible "infrequently" or "never," with a vast majority naming Sunday morning worship as the main resource for their biblical knowledge. The sixteenth-century Protestant Reformation fought existing religious and cultural norms to make the Bible available and accessible to lay readers. In a remarkable "reverse Reformation," many churchgoers today seem quite content to return the primary reading, study, and interpretation of scripture to their pastors and educators.

In his recent study of the religious disposition of baby boomers,

Wade Clark Roof concludes: "Many in these generations [those born after World War II] know very little about specific teachings, or how one faith community differs from another; many just nominally involved within churches, synagogues, and temples find it difficult to articulate what they believe. That is to say, many of them are not very well versed in religious scripts and moral codes, even when they continue—as is the American custom—to claim some affiliation with faith communities."[43] This phenomenon is particularly problematic for theological traditions that place a heavy emphasis on the authority of scripture in faith and practice.

The unfamiliarity with the language of Zion and the abdication of the study of the Bible by the laity is resulting in some ominous consequences for the church. When the Bible is not seen, first and foremost, as the Book of the people, intended to reveal the love and purpose of God to all the world, then it can easily devolve into a secret code book, a Gnostic[44] compendium, whose mysteries are unlocked and known by only by a select few. Clergy, and those few church members who study scripture in some depth and possess a keener facility with the biblical language, can lord their exclusive knowledge over other members in the congregation. With congregations today filled with people who are largely unfamiliar with scripture, it is tempting for those "in the know" to teach, preach, sing, and pray using biblical stories, characters, allusions and metaphors that bring joy to "the elect," but otherwise leave most people untouched or scratching their heads and looking for a translator or, more likely, closing the exit door behind them.

Even more serious for Christians who do not read and study scripture is their vulnerability to cynical secularists who create false dichotomies between faith and science and well-intentioned biblical literalists who, ironically, create similarly false dichotomies as the secularists they condemn. Cynical secularists and biblical literalists both simplify the Bible and posit naive readings of biblical passages that a critical reading of scripture simply will not support. The First Letter to Timothy contains a warning pertinent to secular and biblical literalists. Critical of churchgoers who spend endless hours in idle religious speculation rather than in dedicated service and study, 1 Timothy observes: "Some people have deviated from these [sound Christian doctrines] and turned to meaningless talk, desiring to be teachers of the law, without understanding either what they are saying or the things about which they make assertions" (1 Tim. 1:6–7 NRSV). Too many people, in and out of the church, are engaged today in meaningless talk because they have either abdicated the study of scripture to the "experts" or they read it with an uncritical simplemindedness.[45] A prime example of oversimplifying the Christian faith occurs as respondents across the United States would frequently confess: "I'm not sure what the Bible says about that, but I believe such and so."

What contributes both to this contemporary biblical gnosticism and to the overall decline in biblical knowledge and understanding among church members? Apparently, some church members view the Bible as they view the operating manual for their computer, as something it takes an "expert" to understand and not necessary to use except in the event of a technical emergency. As long as churchgoers can turn on their computers, practice basic word processing and log onto the Internet, why do they need to know about operating systems or databases or hard drives? Similarly, as long as they can reduce the Bible to a workable set of moralisms, or preferably, let the resident biblical "expert" dispense doses of biblical wisdom, then they see little value in learning the Psalms or deciphering the prophets or puzzling over the parables.

Clergy contribute to this unfortunate diminishing of the role of the Bible and biblical language in faith and practice by agreeing, whether gladly or unknowingly, to be the seraphim of scripture. Armed with tools in Hebrew and Greek, a seminary degree, and experience serving the church, clergy too easily become self-appointed Sunday morning specialists, or they are drafted to be the official conveyers of all biblical knowledge for a congregation. Whereas a suitable respect for a pastor's biblical knowledge empowers the educational task of the clergy, any assumption that the Bible belongs mainly in the hands of the clergy results in an impoverished faith and language among God's people and in a potentially dangerous abuse of their calling by the clergy.[46]

In chapters 1 and 2 we witnessed at least an overt "decline of denominationalism,"[47] recognizing that many who come to church today tend to do so with no conscious allegiance to a particular denomination or theological tradition. Yet we also saw that people often stay in a particular Presbyterian congregation due to a typically undefined appreciation of the specific theology, governance, and worship practices of the Presbyterian Church (U.S.A.). The third question of the group interviews was intended not only to discern the particular Christian beliefs of the participants, but also to reveal how well they could express the Reformed/Presbyterian theological emphases of their Christian conviction. The third question followed the format of personal inquiry begun in the second question: "The same acquaintance who asked you about the Christian faith goes on to inquire, 'I drive down the street and see Baptist Christians and Catholic Christians and Methodist Christians. I notice that you are a Presbyterian kind of Christian. Can you tell me two or three of the essentials of being a Presbyterian kind of Christian?' How would you respond?"

A surprising number of those interviewed did not even attempt an answer to this question. The following comments are indicative of comparable remarks made nationwide:

I'd probably say, "Well, you know, I don't really know myself. I've chosen this particular church. I'm not a good person to ask."

There are really significant doctrinal differences between the Catholic and Protestant traditions, but once we're in the Protestant arena, the differences are much less significant.

I've been a church shopper much of my adult life, so I'd tell the person that it doesn't really matter what you believe.

Suzanne, a new Christian from Alexandria, voiced a common response to this question. She said: "My answer would probably be, 'We have some sort of stand on predestination, but I couldn't really tell you what it is.'"

Many active churchgoers in Presbyterian Church (U.S.A.) congregations found the third question either too daunting or irrelevant. New Presbyterians and new Christians struggled most with this question, often responding with a significant and awkward period of silence. Most respondents could venture some broad generalizations about basic Christian concepts, but few could name any distinctive hallmarks of Reformed/Presbyterian thought.

Lifelong Presbyterians were most likely to use Reformed theological concepts in their responses. Etta, a lifelong Presbyterian from Raleigh, struck a common Reformed theological chord when she said: "Presbyterians believe that God is the sovereign One and God picks us. He's the One who starts all the stuff." In Chicago, Ernie, another lifelong Presbyterian, stressed the importance of the shared ministry of clergy and laity in Reformed thought: "Presbyterians do not worship clergy, but recognize that God calls both clergy and laity to accomplish His purpose." Christopher, an elder from New York, stressed the Reformed doctrine of the grace of God: "Presbyterians acknowledge the abiding grace of God and remember that they are forgiven not by what they do, but as a free gesture of the grace of God." Sib, another lifelong Presbyterian from Chicago, added: "An important part of being Presbyterian is thinking about grace—that it isn't our efforts, our works, that get us to God. It is because God found us first." Though typically the ablest in articulating Reformed/Presbyterian beliefs, more than a few lifelong Presbyterians in the study conceded: "I've been a Presbyterian all my life, but I can't really tell you what Presbyterians believe."

In general, active churchgoers express a genuine appreciation for the freedom of inquiry and conscience in the Reformed/Presbyterian tradition. Fowler, a new Presbyterian from Alexandria, said: "I especially like that you are encouraged to question and are not expected to know all the answers." Most respondents felt that Presbyterian beliefs deemphasize guilt and downplay the judgment of God. Largely missing, though, from their responses were comments on human nature, sin and evil, repentance and salvation, justification and sanctification, the work of the Holy Spirit, the person and work of Jesus, and the theological foundation for the church. Only one person in the study affirmed the old Reformed acronym TULIP,[48] which other respondents rejected for its theological reductionism.

In chapter 2 we saw the challenge before churches today to teach members the language of Zion and of their particular theological tradition. Ironically, most congregations in the study typically require only a cursory introduction to the Reformed/ Presbyterian heritage and tradition for new members at their point of entry. Since a majority of new members come from other than a Reformed/Presbyterian background, these congregations are growing with members who may intuitively appreciate the strengths of their adopted theological tradition, but who are woefully ill-equipped to embrace and to use it as a source for understanding God, themselves, and God's world. Nor are they prepared to articulate to others the major tenets of the Christian faith and Reformed tradition.

Presbyterian scholars Coalter, Mulder, and Weeks offer an astute analysis of the status of American Presbyterianism and an accompanying challenge:

Perhaps the most difficult task . . . is to recognize the opportunity that the church confronts in this confusing era. The successive disestablishments of American Protestantism—legally, religiously, culturally—means that mainstream Protestantism has lost its dominance over American culture. All churches must recognize that they now stand in competition with a secular culture. If there is a mainstream any longer, it is not defined by religious or cultural hegemony but by the willingness of these churches to proclaim, without being ashamed, the wholeness of the Christian faith, rather than accent any of its extremes.

American Presbyterians have been central actors in the drama of mainstream disestablishment in the twentieth century, and they could be major figures in the reforming of this tradition. Central to this task will be the recognition that this dark night of the Presbyterian soul offers us a new freedom, a liberation from the need and desire to establish a Christian America or Christendom again. The challenge is to become a church that remains open and responsive to the needs of the age but does not lose its bearings—a church with equilibrium.[49]

If a church with equilibrium denotes a body of believers who understand the fundamental concepts of the Christian faith as seen through a Reformed theological lens,[50] this study of six healthy, vibrant and growing Presbyterian congregations leaves the church today with an even greater challenge than that stated by the authors above.

Only the most optimistic observer can look at the Presbyterian Church (U.S.A.) today and describe it as a church with equilibrium. Conservative coalitions call for biblical, theological, and confessional standards in a futile attempt to resuscitate an idealized version of the American Christendom of the 1950s.[51] Meanwhile, progressive coalitions of Presbyterians call for an openness to biblical interpretation and a diversity in theological expression and espouse minimal standards for church membership. These progressives also advocate the localization of ordination which may appeal to decentralizaling societal trends, but often leaves the church with an ill-defined and disjointed self-understanding and mission. In addition to this long-standing theological divide within the church, the breadth of this divide has expanded in recent years with the proliferation of what Robert Wuthnow terms "special purpose groups."[52]

Art Ross, pastor of four-thousand-member White Memorial Presbyterian Church confessed a weariness with the current lack of theological equilibrium in the Presbyterian Church (U.S.A.) and the rigid and harsh nature of church rhetoric. He said: "I grieve over the things that continue to polarize us. . . . It's the tone of the disagreement that I grieve over the most. My sense is that many of us find our fulfillment and our challenge in the local church rather than in the higher governing bodies. We're committed to the Reformed tradition, but we're just really not interested in getting into a bunch of fights." This analysis was reinforced by lay members across the denomination who praised the strength of their particular congregation, while expressing concern over the rigid rhetoric used across too much of the church today. Church leaders deceive themselves when they see little harm in the vehement rhetoric used to portray their theological opponents. Respondents who were new members of a Presbyterian congregation frequently spoke well of the way difficult issues are debated and differing positions are respected in their congregations, but even more, they applauded the way their church leaders refuse to vilify other Presbyterians with whom they differ. Members of the Calvary Presbyterian Church in San Francisco praised efforts by their pastor Laird Stuart, the moderator of the Covenant Network—a group of churches and Christians in the Presbyterian Church (U.S.A.) seeking a more expansive understanding of ordination, human sexuality, and related issues—to maintain an open dialogue with the Houston-based leader of the more traditional and conservative Presbyterian Coalition. This conciliatory effort—all too rare today—stands out as a bold attempt to bridge the great theological divide within the Presbyterian Church (U.S.A.), a vital step that many others will need to take to achieve a church with equilibrium.

Current intrachurch battles in Protestant denominations resemble something of the proverbial shifting of chairs on the deck of the *Titanic*. I do not intend to suggest that the church of Christ Jesus has been gutted by an iceberg or can be destroyed by doctrinal squabbles, but these divisions work against the church's basic identity as a community of reconciliation. In one of Paul's most eloquent descriptions of the essence of the church's ministry, he writes: "In Christ God was reconciling the world to himself, not counting their trespasses against them, and entrusting the message of reconciliation to us" (2 Cor. 5:19 NRSV).

In addition to their corrosive effect on the church's mission, these battles also deplete the church's energy and creativity and keep it from finding new ways to engage generations of Americans for whom the church is but a curiosity, and the Christian faith only an historic artifact. How can the church ask its members to address the questions of an ill-informed or dubious public unless it redirects the vast resources now spent on "winning" intrachurch doctrinal and ecclesiastical contests? Church members are largely silent before the claims and inquiries of our secular society, not so much because they lack a Christian faith, but because the church has not prepared them to speak intelligently both about the claims of Christianity and of today's proliferation of "isms," from pluralism to deconstructionism.

The church today struggles to live and work effectively within a secular and post-Christian society since many of its members possess only a modest and basically intuitive appreciation of its Reformed/Presbyterian tradition. For church members to serve as faithful disciples of Christ Jesus in the twenty-first century, they need to understand the basics of Christian thought, particularly as seen through a critical reading of scripture aided by insights of the Reformed theological tradition. They also need to know from whence they come. Ted Wardlaw, pastor of the Central Presbyterian Church in Atlanta, offered this telling observation about the growing numbers of young adults attending Central: "They appreciate being a part of something older than they are. Since many members of Presbyterian congregations today bring with them a marginal knowledge of and commitment to the Reformed/Presbyterian tradition, they need to learn the history of Presbyterianism. They need to do so not because it is always a proud and illustrious history, but because they cannot understand where their church has come from, where their church is today and where God is leading their church, without an appreciation for its denominational and theological heritage."

When in an anxious state about decreasing membership, congregations do themselves no long-term favors by deemphasizing their denominational and theological identities. No good purpose is served when congregations downplay the unique history, theology, liturgical practices, and polity of the Presbyterian Church (U.S.A.). Even when faced with a shortage of clergy to serve congregations, presbyteries do the denomination no favor by ordaining a significant number of candidates from nondenominational theological institutions, especially when many of those graduating are relatively new to the Presbyterian Church (U.S.A.).[53] It is tempting to mistake the sociological fact of what Wuthnow and others call a decline in denominationalism as a mandate to discard the relic of denominational identity or to fixate on one era of the denomination's identity as normative for all time. Both options lead to unfortunate and ultimately tragic consequences for the church, because both options mistakenly assume that this current sociological phenomenon must result in the diminishing of denominational and theological identity, rather than its ultimate invigoration.

Surely one measure of any vital and vibrant Christian congregation today is the depth of biblical and theological knowledge of its members.[54] Any congregation that seeks to maintain a faithful equilibrium cannot allow the winds of secularism to diminish the value of a highly informed faith, or specialization to confine biblical and theological study and interpretation to a qualified few. Members, especially new Christians and those new to a particular theological tradition, need to hear the biblical story told with critical clarity and arresting passion, so they will not grow embarrassingly silent when asked: "What do Christians believe?" In addition to the language of Zion, members of Christian congregations today need to relive debates of the early church councils, explore the spirituality of medieval Christianity, study the theological issues raised in the Reformation and Counter-Reformation, listen to the great Enlightenment thinkers and sit at the feet of post-Enlightenment thinkers. Without such a deliberate and expansive educational effort at local, regional, and national levels, any talk of a church with equilibrium will remain a distant dream.

In the next chapter we will look at the role prayer plays for churchgoers who no longer look to the church as the sole dispenser of spiritual insight. We will also explore the remarkable phenomenon of the current fascination with spirituality in the United States while church commitments decline. Sociologist Robert Wuthnow makes this observation about spirituality in America today: "In addition to their places of worship, many Americans now find inspiration at counseling centers and from popular authors and spiritual guides. Growing numbers of people shop for spirituality at New Age and recovery bookstores or pick up spiritual tips from films, talk shows, and news specials on television."[55] In chapter 5 we will look at contemporary understanding of prayer and spirituality as we listen to Christian voices speak of the simple stillness of a mountain stream, spiritual practices in people's homes, and the quiet solemnity of a packed Sunday morning sanctuary.

Chapter 5

Why They Pray

Spirituality and Skepticism

One day the disciples of Jesus drew near and asked him: "Lord, teach us to pray, as John taught his disciples" (Luke 11:2 NRSV). As lifelong Jews, these disciples were no strangers to a daily regimen of prayer. Yet as they witnessed the spiritual discipline maintained by Jesus, they sought a deeper dimension to their own prayer life. In response to their petition, Jesus taught them what has come to be called either the Lord's Prayer or the Our Father.

I suspect that if modern-day disciples of Jesus were to draw near to him today, they would expand upon the early disciples' request and ask: "Lord, also, teach us to be spiritual." Churchgoers and non-churchgoers alike are fascinated with the topic of spirituality. Books on spirituality fill the shelves of booksellers today, and not just Christian bookstores, but university and seminary bookstores, both in the United States and abroad. Recently, Robert Wuthnow and Wade Clark Roof have each written books that study religious life in America today. Wuthnow traces the changing understanding of spirituality in America since the 1950s. About the current rage of interest in this subject he writes: "Judging from newspapers and television, Americans' fascination with spirituality has been escalating dramatically. Millions of people report miraculous interventions in their lives by such forces as guardian angels who help them avoid danger and spirit guides who comfort them in moments of

despair. . . . Some observers proclaim that the dry spell of secularism is over; others wonder whether 'spiritual' has become synonymous with 'flaky.' "[56]

Roof builds on his earlier book, *A Generation of Seekers,* and
explores the spiritual values and assumptions of the baby
boomers. He sets the current fascination with spirituality in an
important social and historical context: "The recent rise of the
'spiritual' as a category of popular religious idiom cannot be
understood apart from considerations of religious and cultural
power. In periods when religious establishments enjoy social
prestige and cultural capital, and thus exercise strong monopolies,
the term appears to languish. . . . In the early 1960s the word 'spiritual' was conspicuously absent in the public arena: religious
language and social ethics captured the day, prompting theologian
Paul Tillich to speak of 'the almost forbidden word "spirit"' and
of the spiritual dimension of life as 'lost beyond hope.' "[57]

A renewed interest in spirituality is not limited to North America. Norman Shanks is the current leader of the Iona Community,
an intentional Christian society based in Scotland, consisting of
believers across the world committed to observing the Rule[58] of
this nonmonastic, nonresident community. In his book *Iona:
God's Energy,* Shanks exposes a dark side to the current fascination with spirituality, both by believers and the religiously curious: "Spirituality is very much in vogue these days, almost
something of a growth industry: the interest in personal development is in a sense the semi-respectable face of the prevailing individualistic, rather introverted ethos of our times. There is a rich
vein to be tapped by those who set themselves up as quasi-con-
sultants, professing expertise in this field!"[59]

The subject of spirituality evokes skepticism among active
churchgoers as well. Mickey, a lifelong Presbyterian from New
York City, said: "The term makes me wonder what it means
because it's used rather like salt and pepper, to spice up a sentence." Craig, a new Christian from Atlanta, objected to the casual
use of the word spirituality: "A lot of people use that term as a
cop-out. They say, 'Well, I'm spiritual,' but they don't have to
define what that means. They can just say, 'Well, I'm a spiritual

person and I have my own spiritual time and I just do spiritual sorts of things.'" Rusty, a physician from a congregation in San Francisco, offered a similar sentiment: "A lot of times when I hear that word, it's from people who have had a bad experience in the organized church. They'll say, 'I'm spiritual, but I don't necessarily like organized religion.'" Ben, a lay leader in his congregation in Atlanta, scoffed at certain notions of spirituality: "I've heard too many times, 'Well, I'm spiritual but I'm not religious. I'm spiritual but I don't want to come to church. I don't want to get up on Sunday and be there, but I'm really very spiritual.'" These comments from longtime and new Christians suggest an uneasiness when the concept of spirituality is reduced by a wider, often unchurched society to mean narrow, self-serving introspection.

For good or ill, large numbers of people today inside and outside the church are on spiritual quests.[60] Some spiritual quests lead people to return or make their first visit to the alien world of a local Christian congregation. Increasingly, though, spiritual quests occur in quiet isolation outside Christian congregations. Today, congregations find themselves in the peculiar position of spectators, watching while active and faithful members worship and serve, but then go other places for counsel in the pursuit of spiritual enlightenment. A major reason behind this shift away from the congregation as central locus for spiritual development is suggested in this excerpt from Wuthnow: "[A] profound change in our spiritual practices has indeed taken place during the last half of the twentieth century. . . . A traditional spirituality of inhabiting sacred places has given way to a new spirituality of seeking. . . . people have been losing faith in a metaphysic that can make them feel at home in the universe and . . . they increasingly negotiate among competing glimpses of the sacred, seeking partial knowledge and practical wisdom."[61]

The scattered, extra-congregational, and typically private approach to spirituality so prevalent in current practice can easily result in a hodgepodge of disparate understandings and competing definitions of the subject.[62] Late in the group interviews, participants were asked a two-part question about spirituality. Part One asked: "A popular term today in and outside the church is spirituality. What do you hear when someone uses that term and what do you mean when you use it?" Responses to this question follow and cover a spectrum of understanding about spirituality today.

Spirituality in American Religious Life

Some American churchgoers search for spiritual meaning by reading the growing number of volumes being written about Celtic spirituality. The ancient Celts did not stress an escape from this world to discern God's mysterious presence. Instead, they pointed to God's mysterious presence in the midst of the realities of everyday life. Norman Shanks explains: "This was based on a perpetual sense of the presence of God, on the view that God is to be encountered not only in the beauty and peace of nature in isolated places, but also in the immediate, rough-and-tumble, in the very middle of life. . . . It would be hard to imagine a spirituality more down to earth."[63]

Though Celtic spirituality is popular today, and may sell large numbers of religious books and meditative tapes, by contrast, most churchgoers possess a far more otherworldly understanding of spirituality. Willie, a new Christian from San Francisco, offered this most un-Celtic definition: "Spirituality is basically operating on the level of things you can't see, things you feel, things that aren't physical—it's a dimension that's something of a challenge for most of us in these days of science where everything is so provable or demonstrable. Maybe that's why it has such an appeal, because it is mysterious, intriguing, and a challenge." Jan, a new Christian from Alexandria, strayed the greatest distance from the Celtic tradition when she said: "Spirituality is moving to a slightly higher place in my conscious thought, however temporarily, in the conduct of my prayer and my conversations with God. When I think of spirituality, I think about that part of me which is here, but not of this earth, and will at some point end what we call time." Jean, a member of the same congregation, added: "Spirituality is that which transcends the world, the everyday," while Lee, a lifelong Christian from San Francisco, asserted: "Spirituality is something that gives substance to your life, totally unrelated to the material world."

Not all churchgoers today equate spirituality with a search for or an encounter with God. Some see spirituality as synonymous with getting in touch with their internal natural powers. Allison, a lifetime member of her congregation in San Francisco, explained: "I wouldn't necessarily associate spirituality with religion or God or a Higher Power, because I think there are spiritual experiences that don't require such an association, like yoga or meditation." Eleanor, a member of the same congregation, added: "I think there is a spirit in each of us and all living things and all existence. Spirituality relates to being in touch and understanding that connectedness." Rebecca, a Christian from Chicago, noted a cosmic dimension of spirituality: "Spirituality is understanding that you are not alone, understanding that you are not the sun and the moon and all the planets, but that you are a part of a greater whole."

In contrast, many churchgoers tie spirituality specifically to their understanding of and relationship to God and the Christian faith. In Alexandria, Robbie, a longtime member of his congregation, explained: "I think of spirituality as a continual sense of or dialogue with God—not an every now and then occurrence when you stop and chat, but the sense of something always there." Candace, a member of the same congregation, added: "Spirituality leads me to express my thanks to God. I think of spirituality as an expression of stewardship. It's the understanding that life isn't mine—it's a loan, and so I appreciate it more." In Raleigh, David, new to Christianity and to congregational life, said: "This discussion of spirituality reminds me of that scene from the film *The Apostle,* when the mechanic, who had been going to church over and over again, on this one day, finally gets it. I can remember sitting at the Easter service last year and thinking, 'I finally get the love of God.' Honestly, it was the first time any of this church stuff meant anything to me."

In his first letter to the Christians in Corinth, the apostle Paul tries to explain to the congregation the corporate, interdependent nature of their spiritual gifts. He writes: "In each of us the Spirit is seen to be at work for some useful purpose. . . . Now you are

Christ's body, and each of you a limb or organ of it" (1 Cor. 12:8, 27 *Revised English Bible*). Consistent with the theology of the apostle Paul, many churchgoers understand their spirituality in the context of their involvement in a local congregation of believers. New to her congregation in Raleigh, Brenda commented: "Coming to church and interacting with people who have similar values is a big part of my spiritual growth. It helps to be in a community of others who share similar ideals." Wayne, a lay leader in his congregation in Atlanta, explained: "Spirituality evolves from living and worshiping and praying with other believers, from being in an environment with friends who share a common belief and commitment to grow in that belief."

Other active church members maintain that discussions of spirituality are foreign to their congregational experience. Jeannette, a lifetime member of her congregation in Atlanta, confessed: "I understand social justice far better than I do 'spirituality.' I'm not sure I really understand the concept at all—in fact, it may be a weakness in our churches that we don't address very well." Melissa, an elder in her New York congregation, said: "I don't think of spirituality as a Christian thing. I don't think it's tied up with Christianity or church life. It's certainly not something we talk about here." When asked if they had opportunities in church to discuss their Christian faith and issues such as spirituality, active church members made these revealing comments:

> We don't often have the settings to talk about spirituality and matters of the faith. I've never been in a situation with people where I could even talk about it.

> It has surprised me how unusual this kind of conversation is in the church. The questions and the topics seem like this shouldn't be so unusual.

> I think you can tell from our silence sometimes that it wasn't because we did not have anything to say, but matters of faith and spirituality are things we don't often talk about in church. It made me think about some things I normally don't.

Some churchgoers equate spirituality with the search for life's greater purpose and a heightened inner awareness. Victoria, from a congregation in Atlanta, said: "Spirituality has something to do with searching for the meaning of life. And I think that search is more complex than the church often teaches. Whatever discoveries come from trying to align my behavior with that search is how I cultivate my spirituality." Jennifer, an accountant and a new Christian from Chicago, added: "Spirituality is bigger than Christianity or any denomination. There are a lot of people who have not been touched by organized religion who are still 'spiritual,' in the sense that spirituality is like trying to heighten your conscience." Wade Clark Roof warns about the effect of a too-individualistic view of spirituality: "When spirituality is recast in strictly psychological terms, it is often loosened from its traditional moorings—from historic creeds and doctrines, from broad symbolic universes, from religious community. . . . In its specificity and inward focus the communal dimension so important historically to cultivating spirituality is weakened."[64]

In his study, Robert Wuthnow interviewed one woman whose comments parallel ones made in this study. Wuthnow writes: "She has a new therapist with whom she enjoys talking about spirituality. 'We both know a lot of people in the religious community,' she says, 'but it's not easy in that environment to talk about spirituality.' "[65] In the twenty-first century, the church will continue to compete with a variety of societal definitions of spirituality, in addition to a host of cultural and religious suppliers of spiritual resources in the great "spiritual marketplace."[66] As a community created and sustained by the Holy Spirit, the church cannot afford a timid posture in the marketplace of religious ideas. It must boldly teach biblically informed and theologically sound understandings of spirituality, while providing a rich variety of opportunities for members to discuss, explore, and practice the Christian faith.

The Christian Life
and Spiritual Practices Today

Part Two of the question on spirituality in the group interviews explores the spiritual practices of those active in Christian congregations today. It asked: "How do you enrich your own spiritual life or sense of Christian piety?" In addition, the eighth question gave respondents a chance to delve more deeply into their own spiritual practices. It asked: "To what resources of the Christian faith do you turn in a time of personal need or crisis?" Respondents also were asked in a written questionnaire to state how frequently they read the Bible and how often they prayed.

In *Thinking the Faith,* Douglas John Hall both defines and then stresses the pivotal role of prayer in Christian life: "Prayer is the nomenclature that we assign to our activity as listeners to the divine Spirit. As such, it is indispensable to theology—just as indispensable as is imagination and inspiration to the artist or musician."[67] In our study, most of the responses from active churchgoers as to how they cultivate their spirituality center around prayer. Valera, a lifelong Christian from Chicago, said: "I grow by asking God through prayer. Sometimes you need to stop and listen and give God time to answer." Phil, from the same congregation, agreed: "I grow primarily through my life of prayer." The majority of respondents pray daily and almost all cite "prayer" as the primary resource to which they turn in a time of personal crisis or need.

The Bible is also a major resource cited for spiritual growth and a trusted companion in troubled times. Peggy, in San Francisco, said: "I draw upon the Bible the way some draw upon other members. I have a number of Bible passages that have gotten me through very difficult times. I see the whole history of our faith is just people like me, struggling with their difficulties." In Raleigh, Hazel, new to the Christian faith, explained: "I come from a background that is not religious. One day I picked up one of those daily religious booklets and started to read and connect with it. I also read the designated Bible passages. I really get something out of it as I see how other people weave their faith into their daily lives." Bud, an active Christian from Chicago, said: "I find the Bible to be very helpful in reinforcing the faith. I particularly love the Psalms and the teaching of Jesus that we are not alone. When faced with loneliness and emptiness, it's wonderful to know that we are loved."

Here are some of the responses that best characterized the comfort members gain from a devotional reading of the Bible:

"In times of despair I lean heavily upon the Sermon on the Mount. I don't think I've ever walked away from a reading without feeling better," said Janet in Atlanta.

"I find the Bible very helpful when I am faced with loneliness and emptiness. It is wonderful to read the assurances that we are not alone and that we are loved," said Brice, a lay leader in his congregation in Chicago.

"I always read the Psalms when life gets overwhelming. A young minister first taught me the Psalms and he said that he had once told his grandmother, 'I don't understand the Psalms.' She said, 'I'm not surprised to hear that; you're too young.' I have found that they do mean more to me as the years go by," said Andy, a lifelong member of his congregation in Alexandria.

Though many respondents listed prayer and the Bible as key resources for their spiritual practice, the questionnaires revealed some challenging realities for congregations in the years ahead. In the 1950s, Protestant and Catholic families not only worshiped on Sunday mornings, but many also read the scripture and prayed regularly in the home. Wuthnow writes: "As the middle class expanded, the family placed increasing emphasis on spirituality within the household. . . . Parents were expected to nurture the spiritual development of their children and to set an example for them by praying and reading sacred texts in their presence."[68] By contrast, this study makes clear that at the turn of the new millennium a different pattern has emerged.

Despite their oral testimonies, in the written questionnaires a large majority of respondents indicate no regular reading of the Bible, with most respondents indicating that their only encounter with scripture occurs when they attend a Sunday morning worship service. While some church members practice a regular devotional reading of the Bible, for many churchgoers the Bible remains a literary stranger.

The infrequent reading of the Bible has potentially dire consequences for the church in America's current secular and pluralistic
society. When church members do not know or have only a passing acquaintance with the biblical narrative and the claims of the
gospel, they tend to oversimplify biblical texts by coating predomi-
nant cultural perspectives and rhetoric with a thin Christian veneer.[69]
Old Testament scholar Walter Brueggemann argues that knowledge of scripture can not only challenge facile Christian rhetoric,
but can tutor a church living in an unimaginative, prosaic world with
the language of poetry.[70] A church without this knowledge of scripture limps into God's world announcing a gospel so puny and mud-
dled that it is heard with more apathy and confusion than gladness.

When the church does not know its sacred text, it is destined to
become irrelevant, or worse, to cede the normative interpretation
of scripture to fringe or special interest groups. Douglas John Hall
makes a trenchant comment on this problem: "If, in my attempt to
combat . . . religious simplism, I have quoted the Bible more frequently than any other document, it is because I am not ready to
let that immense treasure house of spiritual wisdom become the
sole property of the biblicistic simplifiers."[71] The membership of
mainline churches is filled with dedicated Christians who, if
taught to read and interpret the Bible critically, could be powerful
communicators for the good will and purpose of God in a world
often duped by biblicistic oversimplification.[72]

Further, congregations that teach members both the content
and responsible ways to interpret scripture give them important
gifts. So equipped, church members can enter into constructive
conversations with the curious and dubious who venture into
sanctuaries today, especially young people who frequently possess, at best, a one-dimensional and stereotypical understanding
of the Bible. Those congregations that teach and cultivate a love
for scripture also help members to develop the fullest expression
of Christian spirituality. Any understanding of spirituality not
based on a careful and responsible reading of scripture is subject
to the whims of the magical and the market expert.[73]

A church whose members do not know its sacred text is also
destined to leave them bereft of a rich resource in times of

personal need and societal upheaval. The church, then, needs to teach people how to read the Bible critically, but also devotionally. John Calvin included the daily reading of the Bible as a major component of the Christian devotional life. Robert Wuthnow reminds us: "The devotional life was meant to influence ordinary behavior by serving, in John Calvin's words, as 'a tutelage for our weakness,' thus providing regularity to one's activities and periodic moments in which to entreat God for strength and to examine oneself."[74]

In addition to the critical roles played by scripture and prayer in spiritual formation, many churchgoers deepen their spiritual lives through their connection with a community of caring people. Jerry, a physician in Atlanta, said: "This church cultivates my spirituality. When our son was in the hospital, the fact that there were people here praying for him, visiting us, and taking care of our oldest son has deepened my faith in God. Any phone call into the web of this church and I would have the whole web available in whatever support I need. Being here has increased my prayer life tremendously." Fran, from the same congregation, added: "There is a lot of comfort in this community, just knowing that there is a huge backup for help in any difficulty. You always know that you have it if you need it." In New York, Rex observed: "There's something very isolating about pain. It's the fact that it's anonymous and it really doesn't matter who you are; it's just part of life that we all go through. I think pain has a way of making people feel isolated and therefore why this community of joy and pain is so vital." Chip, a member of his church choir in San Francisco, confessed: "My default mode when I'm in pain or frightened is to stay home and hide out. If I can get enough nerve to come here, regardless of what is going on in my life, before I can do or say anything, someone will ask me, 'Do you want to talk?' The most important spiritual discipline for me is showing up on Sunday, because everything depends on my being here."

In *An Agenda for Reform*, Milton Coalter, John Mulder, and Louis Weeks suggest ways a church can support the spiritual life of its members. They write: "One way congregations can support families is to help them learn to worship together again. Before the development of the Sunday school, family piety and worship, along with congregational worship, were the primary means of transmitting the faith. It should come as a considerable shock that a recent study revealed that 63 percent of a group of Presbyterian adolescents have never or rarely had family devotionals."[75] Increasingly populated with members new to the Christian faith or with those for whom the church has felt little need to teach the rudiments of Christian faith and practice, congregations must attend to the spiritual development of members beyond the Sunday corporate experience. To create a community of informed and engaged followers of Jesus, congregations need to teach members how to practice spiritual disciplines at home, such as the devotional reading of the Bible, prayer, meditation, and family service projects.

While encouraging the practice of various personal spiritual disciplines by its members, congregations must be clear that spirituality is always a community and social concern. Norman Shanks captures a biblical vision of the social dimension of spirituality when he writes: "We are 'bound up in the bundle of life' with other people, as Reinhold Niebuhr's famous prayer puts it; it is not possible to separate our personal fulfilment from how we look at and deal with others; the realization of our individual identity is to be found within the context of relationships. Our well-being is dependent on the well-being of others; and correspondingly we are diminished by the suffering of others."[76] In a culture that celebrates the independence of the individual, the church promises a more enduring celebration.[77] Christian congregations celebrate the transforming grace of God upon which every person is dependent, and the sustaining interdependence of the body of Christ.[78]

Congregations must also be clear that Christian spirituality rejects the division of life into the secular and the sacred. George MacLeod, founder of the Iona Community, refused to compartmentalize life, insisting that God's Spirit permeates "every blessed thing." Much of the popular religious literature today portrays the spiritual life as essentially a private, sacred search. Norman Shanks provides this important corrective: "It is of course ultimately a matter of balance. To see spirituality in terms of engagement—with

God, with one's inner self, with other people, with the issues of life—over against the tendency, too frequent in contemporary culture, to see spirituality as escape, essentially about self-fulfillment apart from concern with others and the world about us, is not in any sense to diminish the significance either of a regular personal devotional discipline or of the importance, within our own lives, of withdrawing occasionally from the busyness and demands of people and situations around us for solitary reflection."[79] Congregations create communities of spiritual discernment when they teach members the art of reading and interpreting scripture critically and devotionally; when they prepare members to pray in corporate worship, with their families, and alone; when they nurture their interdependent identity; and when they equip members to live faithfully every moment in the presence of the living God.

In the conclusion to their study, Coalter, Mulder, and Weeks make a persuasive argument for why congregations must be intentional about creating communities of spiritual discernment and teaching members to live faithful Christian lives. They write:

> The central challenge before mainstream Protestants is to recognize our cultural and religious displacement and the need to recover our identity as Christians and bearers of particular traditions that contribute to the richness of the Christian family. We are being thrown back on our own resources and on God, who steadfastly sustains and guides us through all the predicaments in which we find ourselves.[80]

Given the tenuous status of Christianity in America and the decline in society's regard for the church, how do Christians live out their faith in an alien and apathetic land? In a society in which the "self" rules, why do people care for anything more than advancing themselves? In chapter 6 we will explore the difference it makes when people in today's society decide to follow Jesus in their chosen congregation, in their life's work, and in their home.

Chapter 6

How They Live

In this chapter we will look at how people live out their faith in an increasingly apathetic, and sometimes antagonistic, cultural environment. We will also explore the difference that congregations can make for their members, for those who will never step inside any religious institution, and for their local and larger community. Though many current scholars and church leaders lament the church's demise and the plight of those who profess to lead a Christian life, in this chapter we will hear voices from churches which are hardly at death's door. We will see vital signs of God's presence in congregations and in individual Christians who are alive and well despite the multiple obstacles of life and ministry in a once-Christian society.

In the Acts of the Apostles, Luke paints a picture of the dynamism of the early church: "All who believed were together and had all things in common; they would sell their possessions and goods and distribute the proceeds to all, as any had need. Day by day, as they spent much time together in the temple, they broke bread at home and ate their food with glad and generous hearts, praising God and having the goodwill of all the people" (Acts 2:44–47 NRSV). Luke is convinced that the Christian faith transforms the lives of individual believers in their churches and in their world. Luke reports that in the early church, people who had previously only hoarded goods now shared them. Institutions that had previously only concerned themselves with survival now served their neighbors in need. For Luke, the Christian faith makes a transformative difference in believers and congregations.

Centuries later, Nile Harper reflects on a renewed vigor among some urban congregations in the United States. He writes: "Vital signs are indicators of life in the body. Urban churches are a significant part of the body of Christ. They have been through a season of distress and decline. In the past decade, there has been a redevelopment of strength and energy in a significant number of city-center congregations. . . . The vital signs that we report are symbolic of the improving health in a growing number of urban churches."[81] Harper then introduces the reader to congregations nationwide in which there are tangible signs of vigorous growth.

The vital signs in congregational life described by Harper vary from efforts to create more culturally inclusive worship, to inventing constructive ways to nurture and mentor children, to promoting the development of public housing. Though often vastly different in theological assumptions and spanning different denominational traditions, these urban congregations share a commitment to make a difference in their community for the sake of Christ. Similar signs of vitality are evident in the congregations in this study, and in the lives of their members.

Reclaiming "Faith Talk" in Congregations

The apostle Paul implored the Philippians, a congregation especially close to his heart: "Live your life in a manner worthy of the gospel of Christ" (Phil. 1:27 NRSV). Later in this epistle, Paul both urged and reminded his friends: "Rejoice in the LORD always. . . . The LORD is near. Do not worry about anything, but in everything by prayer and supplication with thanksgiving let your requests be made known to God. And the peace of God, which surpasses all understanding, will guard your hearts and your minds in Christ Jesus" (Phil. 4:4–7 NRSV). Though written in a vastly different time and culture, Paul's imperatives still speak with a clear urgency. Paul knows that any difference that congregations and their members make to each other or to those outside the church begins by understanding and embracing the difference God has made for the world through the reconciling love of the crucified and risen Christ.

As followers of Jesus, congregations and Christians in any age live to make a difference for Christ in the world God loves. Douglas John Hall makes a critical point for those tempted to turn the church into a club of holy escape from the world or into a club that holds itself morally superior to the rest of the world: "The church is not a little bit of the world that has finally been fixed up, righted. In a real way, the only thing that distinguishes church and world is that the church knows something about the world that it doesn't usually know about itself: that it is greatly loved."[82] How Christians live follows directly from how they are loved, and, in Jesus, God displays the full spectrum of divine love.

In this study, the ninth question in the group interviews was: "What difference does your Christian faith make in the way you live at work, in the community, or at home?" Responses to this question reveal how active churchgoers today wrestle with the correlation between faith and life, how some struggle to articulate the meaning of their faith, and how rarely local congregations provide an opportunity for talking about matters of the faith.

Novelist John Updike offers this cogent thought about the challenges of faith talk in American parlance: "Faith is not so much a binary pole as a quantum state, which tends to indeterminacy when closely examined."[83] In other words, the origin and growth of a person's Christian faith resists both simplistic explanation and concrete definition. However, based on responses to the last question in the group interview, one might conclude that mainline congregations throughout America must prefer simplistic and concrete assumptions and fear Updike's indeterminacy. For when asked: "In the congregations to which you have belonged, have you ever participated in an interview like this that explores issues of your Christian faith," well over 80 percent of respondents in the study said "No."

When asked to assess the value of such faith talk, an equally large percentage of respondents answered favorably. From San Francisco to Atlanta to Manhattan, active churchgoers reflected:

It was a rare opportunity to reflect on matters of the faith. It's much easier for me to share my deepest thoughts in an environment that I consider safe.

This kind of discussion would attract me on a weekly basis. It's wonderful to hear the different perspectives but also to see the common thread.

I appreciated what others had to say, but I was a little defensive when we started. I am not asked very often to think about or to articulate what I believe.

I tread very lightly when I talk with people about the faith. It can be very delicate, as some of the issues we're facing as a church make for tough conversations.

It has surprised me how unusual this kind of conversation is in the church. Questions and topics like this shouldn't be so unusual.

We don't often have the setting or time to talk about matters of faith. I've never actually been in a situation with people where I could even talk about my questions and convictions.

Scholars repeatedly remind us of the tenuous and limited scope of religious understanding among active churchgoers in America. Most, then, articulate a need to teach members the biblical, theological, and liturgical language of the faith.[84] The voices above add an important insight that scholars, pastors, and other church leaders often underestimate. Not only should members engage in faith talk; they want to! Clearly, congregations miss a tremendous opportunity for enriching the knowledge, faith, and practice of members when they do not design and encourage people to participate in a curriculum that allows for basic and advanced courses on how to understand, articulate, and live the Christian faith in an alien culture.

How Christians Live—Faith in Practice

If faith talk is an atypical commodity even in vibrant congregations today, the impact of faith on a believer's daily life is not.

The tension of the last days of Jesus is magnified in John's Gospel. The sense of impending doom clouds each chapter and the reader feels the anxiety of fearful disciples. In this literary context, Jesus speaks these words to his disciples: "Peace I leave with you; my peace I give to you. I do not give to you as the world gives. Do not let your hearts be troubled, and do not let them be afraid" (John 14:27 NRSV). Followers of Jesus still find that their faith affords an inexplicable peace amid life's storms. Neil, in San Francisco, said: "My faith gives me a lighter heart and a sense of peace and calm. In a frenetic business environment, my faith gives me a sense of serenity." In Raleigh, Joni, a new Christian, explained: "There is a great value to having others pray with and for me. It gives me a certain calmness and confidence amid the vagaries of the marketplace." Despite the stress, moral complexity, and greed rampant in public and private life today, active churchgoers increasingly rely upon the presence of God and the presence of a caring congregation to instill in them the peace of God that surpasses all understanding (Phil. 4:4 NRSV).[85]

Scripture cautions believers not to take moral shortcuts in the marketplace, even when these shortcuts are the ways things are done here. Some eight hundred years before Jesus, Amos mimicked the fraudulent rhetoric of Israel's merchants: "When will the new moon be over so that we may sell grain? . . . We will make the ephah small and the shekel great, and practice deceit with false balances, buying the poor for silver and the needy for a pair of sandals, and selling the sweepings of the wheat" (Amos 8:5–6 NRSV). Later, in his Sermon on the Mount (Matthew 5–7) and Sermon on the Plain (Luke 6), building upon the Hebrew prophetic tradition, Jesus insists that one's faith in God necessarily influences one's life in the marketplace, the home, and the community of believers.

Robert Wuthnow suggests that such biblical admonitions often do not influence churchgoers or congregations. He writes: "Reinhold Niebuhr, writing during the heady, self-congratulatory years immediately following World War II when Americans happily took pride in the accomplishments of their economy . . . underscored the growing tendency to legitimate ourselves on purely pragmatic grounds. 'It is natural,' he observed, 'for men and nations to assume that obvious success and obvious power are the proofs of an inner virtue.' . . . We should instead . . . understand our power and plenty either as an accident of history or an unmerited gift of God's grace. Few, it would seem, have heeded Niebuhr's admonition."[86]

To the contrary, this study revealed that many believers struggle daily to lead their business, private, and congregational lives in recognition of God's grace and according to a higher ethical calling. Yvonne, an attorney in Atlanta, said: "In today's business climate, there are lots of opportunities to be dishonest. I trust that the core values that I have learned as a Christian guide me and drive me to make moral and just decisions." Rod, a new Christian in San Francisco, explained: "My faith gives me perspective at work to stay out of the muck, or at least not to take the muck home with me." Lynn, a deacon in her congregation in Manhattan, confessed: "When there are situations with questionable business ethics, my faith gives me the ability to speak up about it—not without fear—but with a manageable level of fear, instead of being overwhelmed by it." In Chicago, Dexter explained the relationship between faith and practice: "Two things about my Christian faith impact me each day at the office. When someone asks me to do something totally unreasonable, I try to remember, 'Hold on to the good.' And, throughout the day, I try to remember, 'Honor all of God's children.'" Jenny, an emergency room nurse in a downtown hospital in Raleigh, said: "I work with different people every night. Through the years, I have established a certain code of conduct, which I now realize is based on Christianity and is based on my ethics as a Christian." J.P., also from Raleigh, said it with simple eloquence: "My faith helps me take the high road more often than not."

Churchgoers rely on their faith to guide them through more than the ethical complexities of the workplace. Their faith also affords a sense of perspective amid the multiple demands placed upon them at work, by society, and within the family.[87] Pat, in Atlanta, said: "I draw upon the indirect guidance of the church in raising my children. It isn't somebody telling me how to be a parent or run my life; it's just giving me a few things to hold on to—

a context within which to live that makes me a much saner parent than I think I would be on my own." Tyrone, a member of the same congregation, added: "I'm usually patient with my children, which I'm not sure I would be if I didn't have all of these role models of all these wonderful moms and dads here at the church. Watching how good they are with their children makes me realize that I can be that way too." Nan, an attorney on maternity leave in San Francisco, reflected: "My faith has helped me through a major life transition. If you're used to an achievement diet, you are in for a rude awakening when you stay home with young children. I think my faith has helped me reassess what really matters." Alexander, a corporate attorney in Alexandria, explained: "My faith keeps me from working too much. It brings me home for supper with my family, for example, rather than spending the extra billable hours at work as many of my colleagues do."

Even more important to many churchgoers is that their Christian faith establishes a solid theological foundation for personal and public life.[88] Teaching a crowd of followers on a Palestinian mountain, Jesus urged: "Do not worry about your life, what you will eat or what you will drink, or about your body, what you will wear. . . . If God so clothes the grass of the field, which is alive today and tomorrow is thrown into the oven, will God not much more clothe you?" (Matt. 5:25, 30, au. trans.). Morgan, a hospice nurse in Chicago, reflected: "I work in a hospital, often with people who are terminally ill. My faith helps me to offer families a calming presence and a confidence that the body is not all there is." Active churchgoers in this study routinely integrate theological convictions like Morgan's into their own personal and public lives. They observe:

> Whenever I find myself in a compromising or anxious situation, I draw upon my faith, what was spoken from the pulpit in the past and what I have learned from other members and it reminds me why I am here.

> When I get too far off base, something goes off inside me and I remember something I learned in a sermon or a Bible passage I read or a word of wisdom from another member here.

I rely on my faith to make me more tolerant. There are a lot of different people in the world and there is not much you can do about that. My faith keeps reminding me that I am not the center of the world and that other people weren't put on this earth to make me happy.

My Christian faith makes me examine my motives for what I'm doing. That's really when I feel challenged by my understanding of the Christian life, because it often leads me to change my choice, or at least to be honest about the choice.

In his first letter to the congregation in Corinth, the apostle Paul urged members of that congregation: "Be imitators of me, as I am of Christ" (1 Cor. 11:1 NRSV). The New Testament contains repeated admonitions to believers to model their public and private lives after the example of Jesus. Such modeling is not based upon naive assumptions that believers can either know the mind of Jesus or replicate the choices that he made. It does assume, though, that believers will make every effort to achieve a congruence between what they say and what they do in the name of Christ. Gant, an elder in his congregation in Atlanta, said: "I feel like I'm an advertisement for Christianity. Any professed Christian is. So, I don't want people to be able to say of me, 'Oh, there's another person who walks around talking about God, but look at the way he treats his workers.' To be a Christian means I must comport myself in certain ways, and one of them does not include bad behavior, either personally or professionally." Christine, in San Francisco, commented: "My faith leads me beyond being a good or fair person. It leads me to be a witness to Christ in more than my words, but in every form and fashion of behavior."

In addition to providing an internal balance, an ethical framework, and a model for daily living, for many churchgoers, the Christian faith is a source of enduring joy. Joy is often equated with happiness in American parlance, but novelist Frederick Buechner notes a critical distinction: "Happiness turns up more or less where you'd expect it to—a good marriage, a rewarding job, a pleasant vacation. Joy, on the other hand, is as notoriously unpredictable as the one who bequeaths it."[89] Counseling his disciples about his impending arrest and execution, Jesus comforts them with this promise: "You have pain now; but I will see you again, and your hearts will rejoice, and no one will take your joy from you" (John 16:22 NRSV). Arnie, an elder in his congregation in San Francisco, confessed: "I get a sense of joy from my faith every morning. I wake with an undying sense of gladness for each new day." Garry, a new Christian from the same congregation, explained: "The joy that I have in my personal life is a gift from God that carries over into my professional life." Describing how his internal sense of Christian joy directly influences how he lives, Jerry, in Alexandria, said: "No matter how difficult the person may be or how much I detest their position, I try to treat them with respect and dignity."

Active churchgoers struggle to connect what they believe, what they hear in church, and how they live each day. Kitty, new to Christian faith and practice, said: "I struggle with that question [the relationship between faith and practice], because once I leave church on Sunday, within minutes of walking through the doors I basically forget about the church and God unless something bad happens to me and I feel there is a need." The majority of the written questionnaires and frequent comments in group interviews indicate that even active churchgoers often separate their religious lives from their daily personal and vocational pursuits. Tanya, in New York, explained why she finds it difficult to discuss faith-related matters outside her congregation. She said: "It's hard because I do not have any friends or even family members who are Christians. I'm afraid people would look at me as if I had two heads should I talk about my faith. In a secular world, it's tough to talk about faith-related matters."

In our current social and religious climate, even the most vital congregations struggle to help members talk about the Christian faith and understand the illusory, yet intimidating, nature of the wall separating spiritual and secular life. As long as believers and congregations allow this false wall to stand, Christians will miss the overarching presence of God's reign throughout all of life and as a result, they will look for God in all the wrong places. Norman Shanks comments on this artificial sacred-secular dichotomy and the popular lure of spiritual pilgrimages to non-secular remote places: "People come to us [the abbey on the isle of Iona, Scotland] seeking peace and quiet and we try to send them away seeking peace and justice."[90] Later in his book, Shanks expands on his theological understanding of life as transcending categories of spiritual and secular: "The essence of spirituality [which is for Shanks, one's Christian life], the energy and engagement . . . is expressed not just in particular devotional acts but in a whole way of life oriented to the living God, who becomes our constant point of reference and our decisive, focal point of value."[91]

While some churchgoers make few connections between their faith and their daily lives, others tell stories of vocational changes brought about by their Christian beliefs. Beatrice, an early childhood educator in San Francisco, said: "I do something for a living that I believe really feeds the world and serves God. I feel militant enough about serving children that that's the way I believe God has called me to live. Sometimes it's quite a price to pay. It has little status in our society and it doesn't pay anything—especially living in a place like this. I see my job as a call from God." Luis, in Chicago, explained: "My faith led me from being a partner in the city's largest investment firm to find a new life in the world of nonprofits." Most respondents describe less drastic vocational changes prompted by their beliefs, and yet many tell stories of how their Christian faith shapes their work directly and on a daily basis.

Early in the book of Jeremiah, the young prophet protests against God's call to him. When you read the words that Jeremiah preached to the most powerful leaders in Judah, you can understand his reluctance to accept this job. In the fifth chapter of his prophecy, Jeremiah delivers this speech for God: "Scoundrels are found among my people; they take over the goods of others. Like fowlers they set a trap; they catch human beings. . . . They know no limits in deeds of wickedness; they do not judge with justice the cause of the orphan, to make it prosper, and they do not defend the rights of the needy. . . . An appalling and horrible thing has happened in the land" (Jer. 5:27–28, 30 NRSV). Several centuries later, an imprisoned Paul tries to persuade King Agrippa and

Judean procurator Porcius Festus that he has been falsely arrested, but more important, that they too should follow Jesus. Festus responds: "You are out of your mind, Paul! Too much learning is driving you insane." Paul counters: "I am not out of my mind, most excellent Festus, but I am speaking the sober truth" (Acts 26:24–25 NRSV).

In the Bible, faith in God sometimes comforts and consoles believers, but at other times, faith propels believers to speak God's contrary word. Collette, in Chicago, said it plainly: "My faith gives me the courage to speak the truth to power." Chad, an elementary school teacher in Alexandria, explained eloquently: "Some people are not good to kids. They have serious problems and do not want to be exposed and they'll threaten you and take whatever action they can to quiet dissent. If it wasn't for this hero, Jesus, who, without question would have opposed that type of force, it would be difficult for me to do so. Yet I feel that because of my faith, I am blessed with the courage to stand up for what is right." Kelly, from the same congregation, added: "My faith affords me a context in which to make difficult decisions that affect others with whom I work, decisions that sometimes can put me in some real jeopardy."

The Christian faith not only leads people to speak hard words of truth to institutions and people in power, it also leads many active churchgoers to choose lives with a focus alien to the narcissistic, acquisitive ethos of contemporary culture. In the written questionnaire, participants completed the sentence: "I feel most like a disciple of Jesus when . . ." Along with a variety of responses that included worshiping and praying and witnessing, a majority of responses highlight the diverse and many ways that active churchgoers live out their faith among the most fragile and vulnerable people in their communities. A sample of their responses follows:

I feel most like a disciple of Jesus . . .

When I am called out in the middle of the night on a child protective emergency.

When I spend a day each week reading and singing with patients on the Alzheimer's Unit.

When my family spends the night at our local shelter for the homeless.

When I serve as a Stephen Minister and can be a caring presence in the life of someone who is often feeling alienated from her closest friends, and from God.

When I can mobilize the congregation to write "Bread for the World" letters or to march before our state's capital to protest another execution.

When I meet other believers throughout the world on mission trips who care about issues of international social justice.

Beyond the conscious decisions and actions taken by individual believers, there is a collective dimension to discipleship. A potential for more substantial insight and more substantive ministry lies in the efforts of the gathered body of Christ, rather than in the disconnected ministry of a comparable number of individual believers. Educator C. Ellis Nelson proposes an important corrective for Christians who live in a society that overvalues individualism. Nelson writes: "The Christian faith is rooted in congregations. The books of the New Testament were letters to congregations, about congregational life, or, possibly, composed by congregations. . . . Individual Christians, apart from a community meeting for worship and for a sharing of life's experiences in the light of their faith, are unknown in Scripture."[92]

In this study, respondents point consistently to the important role their congregation plays in addressing local and regional socioeconomic issues. Nile Harper observes: "As churches become more and more involved with social justice work, they have also become more politically aware and involved. . . . A number of urban churches have developed sophisticated networks for political action in support of resources for urban redevelopment. The needs and interests of people who have been oppressed, neglected, and under-represented in government policy-making are now more adequately represented and heard. Creating a positive track record through community organizing and redevelopment projects helps attract political support. This is necessary to gain more resources for affordable housing, better schools, adequate health care, and economic development of city centers."[93] Active churchgoers today realize that the creative energy generated when two or three gather in God's name is greater than the sum of an equal number of individual efforts for good.

As local congregations increasingly become the locus for faith formation and the mission work of the church,[94] church leaders face the daunting task of helping members envision and embrace ministries that are best implemented on a national or ecumenical basis. Otherwise, ironically, if ministry is perceived as the sole prerogative of particular congregations, churches will lose sight of the global, interdependent character of ministry precisely at a time when globalization characterizes almost every other aspect of life. Steve, a new member of his Presbyterian congregation in Atlanta, confessed: "This is my private bias, but I think the work of mainline denominations can no longer happen well at any but the congregational level. The day of doing significant ministry beyond the local congregation is over." Steve's voice echoes those of numerous respondents nationwide, as well as noted sociologists of American church life.[95] The views of some ministers in the study parallel those of the laity. They lament a personal fatigue with denominational battles and as a result many find their energies shifting almost entirely to the ministry of the congregation they serve.[96]

Such parochial perspectives and approaches to Christian life in the church, both lay and clergy, reinforce and celebrate the essential ministry of local congregations. At the same time, they fail to acknowledge a scale of ministry that can best occur beyond the efforts of any particular congregation. They look at broken denominational structures and conclude either that they must be repaired or that they are beyond hope. They also look at failed attempts at ecumenical ministry, locally and nationally, and conclude that the only real hope for vital Christian ministry lies at the local level of a particular denomination.

Loren Mead, an Episcopal priest and founder of the Alban Institute, posits an alternative view of the future of ministry at every level of a denomination and between denominations: "The . . .

challenge in building churches for the future is to construct new institutional structures that can carry the faith to generations yet to be born."[97] Mead goes on to contend that despite historic and doctrinal differences, mainline denominations in America will survive and flourish only to the extent that they pool financial and creative resources to instill local and regional trust in national and global ministries. Mead observes: "In terms of basic belief and practice, the differences among the denominations are more and more negligible."[98] In terms of what the denominations are trying to do, the differences are even more negligible. As active churchgoers in this study reclaim their own faith, they strengthen the ministry of their local congregations. These congregations, in turn, must equip these members to value not only the legitimate ministry of their local congregation, but also to value the equally legitimate ministries of congregations joined at the national or ecumenical level.

As churches and denominations enter the third millennium, they must necessarily re-form or they will fall into a state of moral myopia, and fade into social oblivion. The good news is that God's Spirit continues to brood over broken structures and enter into broken lives. The Spirit still challenges the idols of narcissism and ceaseless consumerism, points believers and communities of believers toward the fullness of time and the joy of God's reign, calls people to follow Jesus in word and in deed, raises leaders to guide the body of Christ, and redeems time and all of life for a holy purpose. Like so many other leaders in Christian churches across the world, Norman Shanks asks, "What future does the Church have?"[99] His conclusion reflects the vital hope expressed by active churchgoers in this study: "Some clutch at straws and think the golden days of the past can be recreated. Some see the need for change but cannot discern the way to follow. Some say the Church as it is must die for it to be reborn. But already in all sorts of ways the new Church is already emerging and in this lies the hope and the excitement."[100] In the final chapter we will take a closer look at the potential life and ministry of this emerging church.

Chapter 7

What Next?

Walk into any sanctuary of a mainline congregation on Sunday morning and you will see familiar sights and hear familiar sounds. The pews will be more or less filled; the congregation will stand to sing; the preacher will expound on a biblical text; sacraments will be celebrated and rituals of greeting will follow the service as the congregation exits the sanctuary. Later in the day and throughout the week, these same Christians will say a morning prayer, bless their meals, and call upon the grace and mercy of Almighty God at the close of the day. Seemingly, the churches in America and its members' religious habits remain largely unchanged from the early days of the Puritans in Massachusetts and the Anglicans in Virginia.

While it is true that there are certain enduring Christian forms, rites, and habits, in this study we see that the church in the United States is swirling in a cultural whirlwind. In such times, long held assumptions about corporate and private Christian life prove irrelevant or unhelpful. Tradition constricts the work of Christ to the extent that it freeze-frames the church into one form or period, but it also points the church to trust in the Spirit of God about whom Jesus tells his disciples: "When the Spirit of truth comes, he will guide you into all the truth; for he will not speak on his own, but will speak whatever he hears, and he will declare to you the things that are to come" (John 16:13 NRSV).

As cultures within and outside the church change, some people get nervous and look back for an anchor that will hold the boat steady in a turbulent sea. The Gospel of Mark was written in such a turbulent period. It challenged the early church not to look back or stay put, but to trust in a Lord who goes ahead. Mark's Gospel races the reader through the life of the adult Jesus, with no mention of a birth in Bethlehem or teen years in Nazareth. Once baptized by John the Baptist, Jesus seems to be on a sprint to Jerusalem. The Greek word *euthus,* translated as "immediately," "at once," or "right away," peppers Mark's text, leaving the reader out of breath trying to keep up with Jesus.

In chapter 9, though, there is a strange interlude in Mark's telling of Jesus' forced march toward Jerusalem. Tradition calls it the Transfiguration of Jesus, but the Greek verb is actually *metamorphothei* (most often found in its noun form in English—metamorphosis). It is used here in its passive voice to describe what happens to Jesus. Before the eyes of the gathered church (represented in this story by Peter, James, and John), Jesus is metamorphosized by God. Suddenly, Moses and Elijah stand alongside Jesus, representing the tradition of the law and the prophets. Peter speaks on behalf of those in any age who look for an anchor when turbulence comes, when he says: "This is simply beautiful! This is the way life should be. I'll make three tents; one for you, Lord, one for Elijah, and one for Moses" (Mark 9:5, au. paraphr.). But before Peter can hammer in the first tent peg, Elijah and Moses disappear and a voice sounds from a cloud overhead: "This is my Son, the Beloved, listen to him" (Mark 9:7 NRSV). In other words, you do not discern God's will by looking back or staying put, but by listening attentively to and then responding to the One who still calls women and men to follow him.

Snoopy speaks for many of us who are tempted to stay put in our religious journey. In a Sunday *Peanuts* cartoon by Charles Schulz (Nov. 21, 1999), Snoopy sits at his typewriter composing a new book called *The Dog Who Never Did Anything.* The story begins: "'You stay home now,' they said, 'and be a good dog.'" So he stayed home and was a good dog. Then he decided to be even a better dog so he barked at everyone who went by. And he even chased the neighbor's cats. The story continued: "'What's happened to you?' they said. 'You used to be such a good dog.' So he stopped barking and chasing cats, and everyone said, 'You're a good dog.'" Snoopy retires from the typewriter, lies down atop his dog house, gazes pensively into the sky and concludes: "The moral is, 'Don't do anything, and you'll be a good dog.'" Some sincere Christians advocate such a posture for the church today. They argue: Keep the church fires burning. Wait out the cultural antagonism and apathy until the tide turns. People will come to their senses and return to the church. Other Christians grow hoarse from calling for a return to the good old days and harangue the church to return to some unspecified holier time in the past.

In this study, I met faithful members of the body of Christ who resist both the natural urge to cast an anchor to hold the church in a fixed position, and the tendency to see the future of the church in some idealized version of a reclaimed past. Instead, they listen to our transfigured, crucified, and risen Lord and trust in his Spirit to lead them into new truth. They ask what it means to be the body of Christ in a time when active participation in the church of Christ Jesus is a bold alternative to alluring secular options. In this chapter we will note causes to celebrate, questions to explore, and areas that will require change as the church of the twenty-first century asks itself: What next?

An Invitation to Come

Throughout American religious history, congregations could rely on an "established disestablishment." While American political and religious life had been technically separate, its cultural and religious life were most often complementary. The latter half of the twentieth century saw this historic alliance crumble. Sociologists such as Wade Clark Roof and Dean Hoge tell us that baby boomers left the church in droves in their youth but, unlike prior generations, have not returned in large numbers. To make matters worse, the children and grandchildren of baby boomers often have had little exposure to Christian faith and practice. Many of them think of a Christian congregation and its worship and ministry with the same dispassionate ignorance as an American in the 1950s might have thought of a mosque.

Meanwhile congregations, though often with dwindling memberships, continue to deny epochal changes in the relation of church and culture in America. They often act either as though little had changed or as if the society will soon return to its good senses. Providentially, despite widespread angst and obstinacy in the church, the Spirit of God still leads people to worship and learn and serve in Christian congregations. Yet, as we saw in chapter 1, the reasons people come to church today are often far different than when church and culture were closely wed.

People who come together in congregations to worship, study, praise, pray, and serve make a choice contrary to that of most Americans, even in the most religiously observant geographical regions.[101] Congregations that embrace the necessity to invite people to come, and understand why people do come, and then provide ample and hospitable reasons for seekers to stay, will not necessarily experience a burgeoning membership, but they will enjoy a renewed sense of vitality and purpose.

Throughout the history of most mainline Protestant traditions in America, actively encouraging others to consider the Christian faith and recruiting people for church membership was seen as behavior fitting for fringe denominations which called for an unmistakable choice between Christ and culture. As culture has disassociated itself from the church, mainline congregations are left with habits that no longer well serve God, the church, or potential members. Congregations can no longer open their doors and expect the forces of tradition, family, and culture to lead people there. And when seekers do come, congregations cannot treat them as interlopers and insult them with a constrictive theology that exhibits far more hubris than humility. In addition, mainline Protestant congregations need to rethink their worship schedule. Most congregations offer only one weekly worship hour, and only one day in the week for worship, following an agrarian pattern that no longer reflects the 24-7 work habits of an information-based economy.

Some congregations in this study attract members and visitors too busy to cook and weary of eating alone or dining with family members in front of the television by offering a simple midweek meal. Art Ross describes such a meal at White Memorial Presbyterian Church in Raleigh: "We have a first Wednesday spaghetti supper. No reservations. $3.50 per person. We generally feed around 700 people between 5 and 7 P.M. No program. We come and sit at round tables, and we have different crews that come and work as volunteers. It's a massive undertaking. And it's just a wonderful event. People flock to it. We do it every first Wednesday—even the Fourth of July and Holy Week. It's been a great vehicle for community building."

Some congregations find that a Saturday night or Sunday evening worship service attracts visitors and members whose schedules preclude regular Sunday morning worship. Cary, whose work regularly demands Sunday morning hours, celebrated the decision by Calvary Presbyterian Church in San Francisco to offer a service of worship on Sunday evening. She asked: "When will other congregations 'get it' that Sunday morning at 11 A.M. is simply not an option for a lot of good, believing people today? Nor is it 'the worship hour' from above!" Some congregations appeal to people by opening their doors at noon to provide outstanding music at little or no cost. Fourth Presbyterian Church in Chicago captures crowds of noonday workers along Michigan Avenue through an outreach of music. The Old Presbyterian Meeting House in Alexandria, Virginia, combines fine music and social outreach through its Concerts With a Cause as outstanding musicians perform a free evening concert that is open to the public, with an offering received to benefit a local or national social service effort.

Some congregations fund and operate clinics for the working poor who have jobs but no access to health care. Central Presbyterian Church sits across from the halls of power in Atlanta, and its clinic ministers daily to the poorest and most powerless citizens of the city. Fourth Presbyterian brings tutoring and mentoring skills to children and youth in a low-income area of Chicago. Increasingly, congregations are discovering creative ways to attract and educate people through their Web pages. The January 2000 issue of *The Calling,* a quarterly newsletter for religious professionals, reported that 159 million people are now online in America and that an estimated 70 percent of households have a personal computer. Congregations will miss a growing instrument for welcoming visitors if they choose to ignore or underestimate the present and future influence of Web-based technology.

Vital congregations recognize that they must make visible the message of Christ's redeeming love in contemporary society. They also recognize that many visitors come to them from a nonchurch background and thus do not know the habits and customs of Christian life, much less Christian or denominational history.[102] Hospitable congregations are then intentionally careful with their use of language in worship. When they use such "odd" words as: narthex, chancel, eucharist, intinction, doxology, kyrie eleison, rectory, manse, sanctus, they find ways to explain and interpret these terms. Even as sixteenth-century Reformers insisted that worship and scripture be in the language of the people, so twenty-first century reformers must insist that the church keep the message of the gospel clear to those who come with little or no background in faith, church life, or Christian tradition. When they invite people to turn to Jeremiah 31 or dip bread into a cup or come to Westminster Hall for coffee hour, they need to explain these actions, interpret them clearly, and provide both literal and metaphorical maps.

Congregations can no longer rely on generational evangelism. If the biblical emphasis is taken seriously, they should never have done so. Raymond Schulte makes an important observation about those who come to church today: "Patterns of participation in church have evolved and expectations have reinforced an assumption that church is a place where one goes to receive religious goods and services."[103] With fewer children born to mainline families, and of those, fewer coming to church today, churches face a tremendous temptation to provide an appealing market of religious services for the finicky religious shopper. Congregations and seminaries can easily succumb to the temptation to provide popular yet superficial religious services for their clientele, but they do so at a high price. Schulte asks a critical question for religious leaders of the church today: "What if God has something else in mind? The willingness to name and explore the gaps that exist between the way things are and understandings of the vision God has for the church creates a sense of urgency for change."[104]

People may initially walk through church doors as disconnected consumers in search of religious goods and services, but any congregation that does not both welcome new worshipers as consumers and challenge them to become disciples simply exists as a feeble aid to a disdainful culture. This study, though, suggests that many people come to the church today as more than greedy consumers. They are attracted to churches that state clear expectations for those who would be members rather than churches that provide spectator space for a derivative experience for the religiously curious. Glenn McDonald, pastor of the Zionsville Presbyterian Church in Indianapolis, asks and responds to a question worthy of reflection for any congregation examining its purpose: "What is my deepest wish for those entering our congregation? It is that when it comes to Jesus Christ, they will insist on seeing him for themselves—never being satisfied with somebody else's prayers, somebody else's service, somebody else's experience of the power and presence of God."[105]

Faced with a culture that either disregards the church or views it as alien, some Christians and congregations try to hold onto vanishing realities by turning the church into a religious flea market where you can find whatever spiritual resources you might need at a bargain basement price. Others draw a line in the sand and insist that the way things have always been done in the church is just fine and if people want to come to church, then they had best learn the local language or stay home. These Christians and congregations fail to realize that by their intransigence and lack of hospitality they do not safeguard a vanishing church, but they obscure the new church that God is bringing to life. This study suggests that most people coming to church today are not drawn to congregations that are stuck in a narrow theological or ecclesiastical groove. On the contrary, people are drawn to congregations that maintain a clear sense of their Christian and denominational identity while graciously welcoming, including, and informing all seekers who walk through their doors.

An Invitation to Stay

During much of the twentieth century, denominations were somewhat suspect. Theologian and ethicist H. Richard Niebuhr felt that denominationalism in America spoke to the moral failure of the church. In Niebuhr's analysis, denominations represent the worst of ethnic, racial, and economic division. While Niebuhr's analysis bears continued scrutiny and should hardly be dismissed, in this study I found that denominations play a more lively role than Niebuhr and others would say they warrant. Though seekers are often unaware of the particularities of the denomination to which they belong, this study suggests that it is precisely those particularities that often cause them to remain in a congregation.

Nancy T. Ammerman, who teaches at Hartford Seminary, found that an intentional denominational identity exists most noticeably in rural and southern regions of the country and is closely related to how many members of a congregation grew up in that denominational tradition. Consistent with the current study, she found that many Protestants switch denominations, often multiple times, in the course of a lifetime. The phenomenon of "switching" is far less prevalent in Catholic and African American parishes.

Ammerman notes a common sense of resignation among church members who feel a decline in the role of their denominations. She then studies congregations who take a path contrary to the wisdom of megachurches and church growth "experts." These churches are conscious and careful about establishing and explaining their denominational identity. She suggests an approach consistent with findings in the current study: "Perhaps we need to reopen our dialogue with Niebuhr. These congregations in which distinct denominational identities are being chosen and nurtured do not seem to be the worse for it. Most are vital and growing, and few if any are isolated or hostile to the outside world. Rather than disappearing, their boundaries have been reconstructed in ways that seem to keep them open and connected to a larger world. Unlike the denominationalism Niebuhr feared, they are building distinctions based more on ritual and doctrine than on social divisions. In the midst of a bewildering and mobile world, they have found places to stand. Theirs is an experiment in blending tradition and openness that bears watching."[106]

Throughout the current study, I found that often people stay in churches because of the unique worship, education, and mission perspectives of a particular denomination. Many worshipers come from other denominational traditions or no Christian tradition at all and most cannot clearly identify the distinctive emphases of their denomination. Even so, oral and written interviews reveal that a major reason seekers stay in a particular congregation is its denomination's biblical, theological, and liturgical tradition. Ammerman's insights may encourage important conversations within and between denominations, so that those who first come or return to church life may not be laden with archaic denominational culture-bound accretions, but will benefit from the enduring insights unique to their particular tradition.

The current study also suggests that people stay in congregations in which they are made to feel welcome. Paul instructs the congregation in Rome: "Welcome one another, therefore, just as Christ has welcomed you, for the glory of God" (Rom. 15:7 NRSV). Vibrant congregations recognize the necessity to make ways for new members to find their place in the community of faith. Too many congregations and Christian scholars today write off the world and carve out a special niche for the church as a body of resident aliens.[107] While society may write off the church—and largely has in much of American society today—the gospel Jesus proclaimed requires that the church engage in a persistent creative and loving engagement of the world. It also requires an openness to those who are seeking Christian discipleship and who need room to question, to wrestle, and to grow. Norman Shanks wisely reminds the church: "In a world that is hungry for meaning and purpose, for a sense of priorities and values, it does people no service to pretend that the Christian faith is somehow about arriving . . . rather than a continuing journey of ups and downs through which God will sustain us and Jesus Christ walk with us as he accompanied the disciples on the Emmaus road."[108]

The notion of unchecked individualism, as explored in Bellah's

Habits of the Heart, contends that as individualism has expanded in the United States, community efforts, such as church involvement, have necessarily declined. The current study reveals that growing individualism coupled with culture's disestablishment of itself from the church has led to an interesting phenomenon in the church. Since people are less inclined today than in America's past to join a church because of family or societal pressure or culturally reinforced habits, those who do join often do so at a higher level of intentionality and with strong expectations. Wade Clark Roof says: "Fears that excessive individualism is destroying institutional loyalties are easily exaggerated and distract from its positive values for genuine religious conviction. Individualism also makes possible an affirmation of religious faith, identity, and belonging—as self-chosen. And as a result, people often possess a greater clarity of their own beliefs and metaphysical views as well as a sense of personal accountability; contrary to views that individualism only erodes commitment, it can actually 'tighten,' and not just 'loosen' ties to groups and institutions."[109]

Increasingly, Christians and congregations find themselves living on the outskirts of culture's considerations and reacting against what culture defines as valuable. Consistent with findings in this study is Roof's analysis: "Even among those lacking a good vocabulary for expressing their inner selves, or for whom spirituality is vaguely defined and without much real power to challenge their secular values and assumptions, there is a yearning for something that transcends a consumption ethic and material definitions of success."[110] Congregations that see themselves as more than chaplains to the culture recognize the powerful role they can play in giving members opportunities to explore the rich and varied textures of the Christian faith and to experience how faith can help interpret culture. Far too many of the active Christians in this study reported little or no opportunity to discuss basic Christian beliefs and practices in secure small group or seminar settings. People will stay in congregations that provide a safe and welcome setting where long-term and newer members can raise questions and learn both from faith shared and questions raised. Such settings will also provide opportunities for believers to discuss the complexities of living as a faithful Christian in a culture that knows more of the lore of Santa than of the message of Jesus.

Mark's telling of the Transfiguration of Jesus notes that on the way down the mountain the disciples jockey for a position of privilege in their imagined religious hierarchy. Then they try to prevent nonfollowers of Jesus from healing and get a well-deserved lecture from Jesus about leading a life of discipleship that does not distract others from the faith (see Mark 9:33–49 NRSV). People often come to church today with such an "instrumental" view of Christian life, asking, "What good will it do me to be a Christian? How will following Jesus benefit me? How will church participation help me become a better person?" People stay in congregations in which they learn to move beyond such an "instrumental" view, and begin to see themselves as instruments of God's loving purpose in the world.

People will stay in congregations that also help them realize the joy of belonging to God and to each other. A vital and vibrant congregation of the twenty-first century will aid people who say "I go to church" to think and believe "We are the church." Paul gets the order right in his first letter to Corinth: "Now you are the body of Christ and individually members of it" (1 Cor. 12:27 NRSV). Once embraced, members and congregations will find their God-given purpose in giving themselves heart, soul, and mind to serve others in a world that is often indifferent and occasionally antagonistic toward the church. Nile Harper suggests that any valid Christian purpose and mission "must go beyond the need to feel good about giving. What is most valuable is active partnership between oppressed people seeking to change conditions of injustice, and other people who are willing to join in a common effort so that equity can be established. . . . Such a calling moves people beyond charity toward greater commitment, wider vision, and more systematic action for justice."[111] People will stay in congregations that recognize that they are inseparably a part of the world God so loves and for which Christ died. Congregations that mainly concern themselves with making members feel good will soon find that this thin theology leads people to look elsewhere as they search for lasting religious truth.

An Invitation to Worship

Congregations establish their identity through educational programs, mission initiatives, and fellowship groups, but nowhere does a congregation establish its identity more definitively than in its corporate worship. Coalter, Mulder, and Weeks contend: "When people become Christians, they join congregations, and besides the Sunday school, worship has the most powerful influence on the growth of individuals in the knowledge and love of God."[112] Findings from the current study suggest that even more than Sunday school, worship is essential to the identity of congregations and the growth and witness of individual Christians.

It should come as no surprise, then, that worship forms and practices are, and always have been, a cause of fierce church battles. One of the earliest worship controversies surrounded, not a debate about the real presence of Christ in the Eucharist, but greed and gluttony at the table. Paul instructs the Christians in Corinth: "So then, my brothers and sisters, when you come together to eat, wait for one another. If you are hungry, eat at home, so that when you come together, it will not be for your condemnation" (1 Cor. 11:33–34 NRSV). From the early church on, worship, because of its great importance, has often been a battleground in Christianity.

As American culture pushes the church to the margins of society and rapid cultural change prevails, church members sometimes react to their declining prestige in society by resisting internal changes, especially any changes in worship. Long term church members were the people in this study most inclined to make statements such as the following:

I don't understand why we need to change what has worked well all these years.

If our worship service was good enough for my grandparents, it should be just fine for my grandchildren.

The truth, though, is that worship in mainline Protestant traditions has changed over time. The Reformed tradition serves as an apt example. Coalter, Mulder, and Weeks explain: "Worship in

Calvin's Geneva did not break radically with the liturgical character of the Roman Mass, except in its emphasis on the sermon. But the later Reformed tradition, especially English Puritanism, increasingly simplified the service to purify it of "Romish" or "papist" elements. A typical American colonial Presbyterian service consisted of singing two or three psalms, the reading of scripture, a long sermon of an hour and a half to two hours, and a pastoral prayer of approximately forty-five minutes."[113] Similar changes have occurred in music within worship. In 313 C.E., the Edict of Milan banned instrumental music, fearing that pagan instruments would lead to pagan influences in the church. Yet by the time of the medieval church, instruments were an integral part of worship. And by the sixteenth century, Luther had welcomed instrumental music into Christian worship. He encouraged the public singing not only of psalms but also of biblically inspired hymns, of which Luther wrote more than thirty. The Folk Mass in Roman Catholic parishes after Vatican II introduced a diversity of music and instruments previously uncommon to mainstream worship in America.

Historically, change has been a given in Christian worship. Why? Because the Spirit of God continues to give God's people new insight, new songs, and new ways to sing God's praise. However, some still fear that changes in worship necessitate a rejection of time-honored liturgical traditions. Tragically, sometimes they do. Some congregations succumb to worshipers' worst fears by making wholesale changes to attract a larger consumer audience. By neglecting the foundational tenets of their corporate worship, they can easily turn worship into an exercise in market sampling, rather than an experience of divine praise.

In 1999 the Episcopal Church in the United States did a self-study called the Zacchaeus Project. It found numerous areas in church life requiring change, but it also uncovered worship practices that were definitional for the denomination. Numerous respondents said, "Because of our Prayer Book, you can go anywhere in the country and feel right at home in the worship services."[114] Congregations that understand the basic worship practices of their theological tradition and clearly interpret these practices to worshipers will avoid the lure of mere relevance at the cost of dismissing the basics.

At the same time, as vital congregations understand the fundamentals of their worship tradition, they position themselves to explore new (at least, new to their worship tradition) worship practices, opening themselves up to new ways to worship God. In her research, Nancy Ammerman found: "What distinguishes congregations where denominational traditions are valued and sustained from those that resign themselves to their 'generic' fate is the way they undertake three key practices of congregational life—worship, mission, and education."[115] In the current study, seekers and members alike appreciate congregations that respect the distinguishing marks of their worship tradition, but are also open to worship insights from other members of the Christian family. In a day when "switching" prevails in most mainline traditions, people join congregations in which they find meaningful ways to worship God that include significant and theologically consistent insights and practices from their denomination's liturgical background.

On a typical Sunday morning, many congregations, particularly in urban areas, will be visited by people from other parts of the world, those of marginal worship experience, and the simply curious. The worship experience can communicate a receptive environment for new and old to praise God or it can do quite the opposite. Vibrant and vital congregations evaluate their worship service regularly. They ask such seemingly simple questions as these:

> Is it clear to visitors where to go for morning worship and are the community's practices made clear as the service begins and ends?

> How does the worshiper pray in worship? Is kneeling or standing or sitting reverently the preferred posture? If so, how do visitors know?

> What do people do when a plate passes by? If you want to write a check, to whom do you write the check and what is a fair amount to give?

> Does the congregation say anything in response to readings or anthems? If so, is there a special formula, and what does it mean?

If the congregation uses prayer books and hymnals, is their use
explained clearly to those unaccustomed to such worship aids?

Congregations that seek to create an informed community of
believers, and try to avoid any semblance of magic, make an extra
special effort to explain the theology and practice of the sacraments.[116] Congregations that assume everyone "gets it," uncon-
sciously limit those who elect to stay. Even worse, they
communicate that worship is for those "in the know" rather than
being an occasion for people "to come to know" their God.

Loren Mead, founder of the Alban Institute, argues: "In the
process of building religious institutions, we have created a power
and ownership structure in which the clergy wields most of the
power. They are now locked in place by customs and laws
intended to preserve the institution. In fact, the 'arrangements'
keep the clergy in institutional power but make it increasingly
impossible for individual clergy to carry out their mandate to be
bearers of the religious mystery, to have religious rather than
institutional authority."[117] Mead draws a sharper distinction than
perhaps exists, but he raises an important issue that surfaces in
modern worship wars. In the current study, active churchgoers
value worship that honors the hard work and unique calling of the
preacher/liturgist, but that also respects the contribution of committed laity, since liturgy is ultimately the work of the people.

When asked to describe the most meaningful component of
corporate worship, people spoke consistently and passionately
about the preached word. Paul explains the saving power of the
gospel to Christians and then asks: "How are they to call on one
in whom they have not believed? And how are they to believe in
one of whom they have never heard? And how are they to hear
without someone to proclaim him?" (Rom. 10:13–14 NRSV). Vibrant
churches recognize the importance of the preached word. They
find ways to help their preachers have adequate time for biblical
exegesis, prayerful reflection, related reading and research, the
final writing of a sermon, and necessary oral preparation. Clergy
sometimes expend hours on tasks that may put them in good stead
with their congregations, but these tasks are often of secondary

importance to the sermon or to the shaping of the worship service. In addition, congregations often hold unrealistic expectations for their pastors, demanding fine preaching but requiring attention from their preachers that other staff or lay members could provide just as effectively, if not better.

The nature and quality of worship is a critical concern, with systemic implications, for the church in a postmodern culture. The proclamation of the gospel for the salvation of humanity requires that those persons charged with and trained for this task recognize the intricacies of biblical hermeneutics, the complexities of today's politics, economics, and ethics, and the congregational context in which they preach. Preachers who see the gospel as simply salve for the soul or as an endorsement for a consumer culture not only miss the thrust of the biblical message, but misguide their congregations as they regularly trivialize the message and meaning of the Christ.

Elizabeth Lynn and Barbara G. Wheeler have recently explored what the public thinks about religious leaders and the seminaries that train them. They conclude: "People interviewed [for their study] consider seminaries invisible institutions that produce leaders who offer little civic or public leadership."[118] Sadly, many mainline churches could be similarly indicted today. The current study reveals a yearning among active churchgoers for prophetic voices from the pulpit, voices that challenge prevailing cultural assumptions with the claims of the gospel of Christ Jesus. And yet too many preachers are so overwhelmed with keeping the institution afloat that they cannot find time to read, to involve themselves in the life of their city or community, and to be still and listen to the guidance of the Spirit of God. As Lynn and Wheeler discovered, too many seminaries model this invisible posture for their students, and the students learn well: "Seminaries are quiet to the point of absence in their local communities. But then so . . . are the religious leaders they train."[119]

In a culture that perceives the church as invisible, corporate worship is the prime occasion for congregations to be reminded of their call to do far more than take good care of their own. Marci, a longterm member of her church in Atlanta, spoke on behalf of numerous laity in this study: "People who are called to be pastors must be able to speak beyond the boundaries of the local congregation. We can easily consume a pastor's time and often do, but we must insist that pastors have a duty to speak to and get involved in the larger community. We need to hear more than soothing words from the pulpit." Congregations need to insist on and provide for the time and resources for those who preach to be biblically astute, theologically sound, and socially engaged.

Since many members today are new to Christian worship or have "switched" from one liturgical tradition to another, the time is right for pastors to share with lay members both the planning and leading of corporate worship. In several of the congregations in this study, lay members do far more than pass out a morning bulletin. They read scripture, write prayers, share the concerns of the community, and sometimes preach. Getting laity involved meaningfully in worship is yet another demand on a pastor's time, at least initially, but it is well worth the investment. As lay members take ownership of the worship of God, they communicate to the congregation (and remind pastors) that worship is not a professional show conducted by the paid stars. They also learn the art of worship leadership, from reading scripture to leading prayers to writing litanies. In turn, they often experience a desire to learn more about Christian worship and to deepen their lives of devotion and prayer.

Whether led by lay members, pastors, or by both, Christian worship faces some significant challenges in the new millennium. Much mainline Christian worship echoes its noisy surroundings. When the congregation prays, it is too often exclusively the voice of the liturgist it hears, rather than listening in silence for the voice of God. Members are asked to meditate on the gifts of bread and wine at the same time they are asked to sing a hymn or listen to a solo or hear the organ play. Throughout this study, active churchgoers asked for more time for a holy silence in worship, not just an absence of sound, but a focused time to "be still and know that I am God" (Ps. 46:10 NRSV). Vibrant and vital worship respects the word of God as it is proclaimed through the preached word, sung and played through congregational, instrumental, and choral music, enacted through the gifts of the sacraments, and experienced through attentive and silent listening for the voice of God.

Perhaps music presents the greatest challenge to meaningful worship in the church today. Even as pastors can no longer assume their congregation will know the story of David and Jonathan, neither can church musicians assume that their listeners will know Bach's B-minor Mass. While the church has a responsibility to teach its members to appreciate fine music as a vehicle for the praise of God, the church also has a responsibility to discern new forms and modes of music that expand the congregation's musical repertoire. The music ministry of the church holds another rich possibility for partnership between pastors, musicians, and lay members, a partnership in which the overall worship experience of the congregation is enriched because of the willingness of worship leaders to see beyond turf battles to the church's greater good. Pastors, musicians, lay worship leaders, and worshipers face the same question asked by an ancient Israelite in Babylon: "How could we sing the LORD's song in a foreign land?" (Ps. 137:4 NRSV). Vibrant congregations will approach that question less as a lament and more as an occasion for renewed thanksgiving and praise.

An Invitation to Believe

In America's religious past, worshipers were most often raised within one denominational tradition and remained in that tradition throughout their lives. So, when congregations received new members, they came largely from other congregations within the same denomination. In each congregation of this study, most new members over the past decade came from other denominational traditions, or with no background in Christian faith and practice at all.

This relatively new phenomenon in American religious life raises competing considerations for the church. First, in the face of declining numbers of members and the resulting anxieties, many congregations have made the act of joining as easy as a credit card purchase. New members are not asked to meet with

governing bodies, nor do they hear what time and financial commitments are suggested, nor are they queried as to why they seek
to follow Jesus in this denomination and congregation. Consistent
with culture's insistence on instant gratification, congregations
often accommodate seekers by making church membership quick,
simple, and painless.

Second, as more people with little or no Christian, biblical, or
theological background seek membership in congregations, how
well does the church serve these people who are quite serious
about their decision by minimizing the entry process? The church
fails itself and the world around it when it does not differentiate a
simple faith from a simplistic faith or when it allows to stand
unchallenged the false dichotomy of faith and knowledge. The
intentional, and often thoughtful, commitment to be involved in
church life and yet the lack of biblical depth and theological
awareness by new and some older churchgoers in this study argue
for a different entry process. People come to church today with a
willingness to learn, to serve, and to give far beyond what most
congregations ask of them. Glenn McDonald discovered that the
problem of expecting only a minimal level of commitment from
church members lay not with the new members, but with anti-
quated or anxious overreactions by church staffs. Now, however,
"after years of experimentation and reflection—and membership
protocols that tended to err on the side of inclusiveness—our staff
came to the conclusion that our membership process could and
should be far more than a perfunctory series of classes."[120]

Third, congregations do a disservice to their members when
they underestimate the cost of discipleship. Three times in Mark's
Gospel, Jesus tells the disciples that he will suffer and die. The
disciples ignore, cajole, and urge Jesus to soften his message. He
doesn't. In the eighth chapter of Mark's Gospel, after rebuking
Peter, Jesus called together his disciples and followers and said to
them, "Whoever wants to save his life will lose it, but whoever
loses his life for my sake and for the gospel's will save it" (Mark
8:35 Revised English Bible). The cost of discipleship has not
diminished in two millennia. In fact, in a culture that no longer
sees itself as a prop for Christianity, discipleship will only

become more difficult in years ahead. The church today often finds itself desperate for new members, but it will not keep them long unless it equips and then expects of new members a life of worship, service, devotion, and learning. To dismiss those coming to church today simply as consumer Christians who desire instant spiritual gratification paints too simplistic a picture. Nor should the church refrain from calling all members to a sacrificial life of discipleship because of the false assumption that consumer Christians will only do what benefits them.

Rarely has the church seen a time when so many new and newer members need and seek out good Christian education opportunities. In several congregations, I found pastors and Christian educators and lay members forming a natural, but uncommon, alliance to plan and provide outstanding educational opportunities. The Fifth Avenue Presbyterian Church in Manhattan offers a lay academy of learning that includes a wide variety of classes in Bible, theology, ethics, Christian living, spirituality, discipleship, Christian movement and expression, and more. These classes are open to the congregation, but also to busy executives at the noonday hour, to commuters on their way home at 5 P.M., and to interested New Yorkers on any weekday evening.

Congregations have too large an educational task before them to settle for educational philosophies and programs based on a church that no longer exists. Pastors and educators must put down their swords of antagonism and work together in an atmosphere of mutual respect and model for their members a collegial learning environment. If worship and mission are to be meaningful, members need to learn the biblical story in which they now take their part. If theology is to make a real difference in the lives of believers, they need to learn the story of their theological tradition. And yet the church must be honest with itself, its members, and the surrounding culture as it teaches members both the content and complexities of their biblical and theological stories. Religious leaders must communicate not only that scripture and tradition matter, but help members understand why.

In her research on congregational life in America today, Nancy Ammerman found: "On the cusp of the twenty-first century, a strange thing is happening. Congregations—not all, but a notice-able number—are choosing to highlight their denominational par-ticularities."[121] The current study also found that many members appreciate the essential ethos of their denominational tradition, but are largely unable to articulate it. Now is the time for church leaders across denominations to ask hard questions about what wisdom their particular tradition continues to bring to the larger Christian communion. New Christians and members new to a par-ticular denomination deserve an educational opportunity that highlights the strong heritage of the particular tradition, is honest about its blemishes, and is respectful and open to insights from diverse theological traditions.

To obscure denominational symbols and to disguise denomina-tional emphases in an attempt to attract new members proves con-trary to the findings of this study. This does not mean that Niebuhr was wrong and that denominationalism should be uncritically cel-ebrated. Garrison Keillor rightly mocks an unexamined denomi-nationalism as he describes one response to the concordat between Lutheran and Episcopal churches:

> I'm a Lutheran, a Lutheran, it is my belief,
> I am a Lutheran guy.
> We may have merged with another church
> But I'm a Lutheran til I die.[122]

In a culture that does not distinguish between a Methodist and a Quaker, or care about internal denominational battles, congrega-tions had best not idolize their tradition and fuel theological and liturgical wars in which most members and the larger society have no interest. Neither should congregations ignore that which has made their worship, education, congregational life, and theology unique. Congregations that honor their theological tradition, are honest about its heritage, and inculcate respect for other religious traditions in and beyond the Christian family will thrive.

Congregations and their educational leaders can easily feel overwhelmed by the immensity of the teaching task before them. The need for biblical and theological knowledge is great, mem-bers' expectations are high, and the available resources are limited.

Even so, the same congregations and leaders should take heart that pews are being occupied less by people who claim to know all they need to know about the Christian faith and practice and more by people who are humbled by how much they need to know. They are people who yearn to discuss their beliefs and wish to lead a well-informed and dedicated life of Christian discipleship.

An Invitation to Prayer

Early in his recent book on the phenomenal popular interest in spirituality in secular America, sociologist Wade Clark Roof writes: "In my judgment, the current religious situation in the United States is characterized not so much by a loss of faith as a qualitative shift from unquestioned belief to a more open, questing mood. Underlying this . . . a set of social and cultural transformations have created a quest culture, a search for certainty, but also the hope for a more authentic, intrinsically satisfying life."[123] Lorna, a new member of her congregation in San Francisco, reflected on her search for meaning: "When I first started to come here, I used to come every Sunday at 10:30 A.M. because that is choir practice time. It was great because I could sit in this beautiful huge building with no one around me, sit there and be alone and listen to the choir go through the steps. Now, I'm there at 10:30, but I am usually the last one out of the building because I'm so busy catching up with new friends."

Even though church and culture are no longer wed in America, as Roof documents, people still search for a more meaningful life. But they no longer limit this search to the church. In the church, more and more worshipers come with models of spirituality gleaned from popular culture, where they have seen what it means to be *Touched by an Angel* and have read about how to have *Conversations with God.* The good news for the church is that if anything, the rise of secularity in America has encouraged a renewed quest for a meaningful life. What will the church say to those who come to church on this quest?

In this study, the word spirituality is most often used to describe private religious experience, set apart from the secular, everyday world. In many mainline traditions, especially in the Reformed traditions, the church has rejected such an individualistic view of the world and the spiritual life. Sociologist Robert Wuthnow sets this issue in context: "Traditionally, the spiritual ideal has been to live a consistent, fully integrated life of piety, such that one's practice of spirituality becomes indistinguishable from the rest of one's life."[124] Holly, a social worker in Atlanta, expresses Wuthnow's thought in another way: "I become more spiritual by becoming more aware of what's going on outside the church. I come to church to put life in focus. And hopefully, I take something away from it, that my eyes are opened to the things that are happening outside. I become more conscious of other people's thoughts and needs and treat everybody with a greater respect."

Confronted by a culture that now lays claim to the concept of spirituality, and a church that is often reluctant to explore this subject seriously, how will the church of the twenty-first century help its members understand and practice a spiritual life? Wuthnow reaches a conclusion fully consistent with this current study: "The shift that has taken place in U.S. culture over the past half century . . . means that attention again needs to be given to specific spiritual practices by those who desire to live their whole lives as practice. . . . Nevertheless, the point of spiritual practice is not to elevate an isolated set of activities over the rest of life but to electrify the spiritual impulse that animates all of life."[125] As new and often unschooled people come to church today, Christian congregations are positioned uniquely to add depth to the popular understanding of spirituality and breadth to the spiritual impulse of its members. In a society fascinated by ghosts, goblins and spirits, the church must point its members to God's Holy Spirit, which leads people to faith, connects believers inextricably with each other, and empowers the church to present the life-transforming claims of the gospel to a culture that now settles for so much less. As Paul reminds the floundering body of Christ in Corinth: "Just as the body is one and has many members, and all the members of the body, though many, are one body, so it is with Christ. . . . Now you are the body of Christ and individually members of it" (1 Cor. 12:12, 27 NRSV).

At this point in American religious life, the teaching ministry of the church and the spiritual life intersect. Congregations are faced increasingly with members who have come to believe that spirituality is a private pursuit for personal spiritual well-being, to be added to their educational, financial, vocational, and recreational well-being. Faced with such misguided theological assumptions, the church must assume three roles to counter and deepen the belief system of its members.

First, the church must teach how to best understand the concept of spirituality. Consistent with the findings of this study, Norman Shanks urges: "Spirituality itself needs to be demystified! It has become ambiguous and confusing, esoteric and precious. It has to be rehabilitated from the connotations of dilettantism and religious tourism that it carries in some quarters and rediscovered as a concept that is fundamental to our humanity and morally neutral."[126] Congregations that help members to grasp and practice spiritual disciplines will unearth a profound inner energy.

Second, the church must guide members to learn that there is no division of worlds, as if when one steps into the church he or she is in one world and when out of the church in another. The Psalmist says it best: "The earth is the LORD's and all that is in it" (Ps. 24:1 NRSV). In the Judeo-Christian tradition life is not an escape from an evil and hopeless world, and sanctuaries are not the special domain of God. A spiritual life is one that seeks to discern the mind of Christ in order to make a difference for Christ in God's beloved world. Congregations then can neither ignore the need to teach and nurture the faith of its members, nor confuse a rich spiritual life simply with personal and private religious pursuits.

Third, the church in the twenty-first century must instruct members about personal and family spiritual disciplines that animate all of life. Certainly, as we saw in chapter 3, worship is a fundamental spiritual discipline of the Christian faith. As congregations examine traditional and new ways to worship, they must be clear that good worship takes work and deserves the best efforts of worship leaders and congregations. If the biblical and theological traditions of mainline churches are even close to God's truth, then it is simply not true that one can worship God just as well on the golf course as on a pew, just as well with scattered, unfocused words of praise rather than in thoughtful and provocative corporate worship. Tom Troeger calls for believers to offer God their finest efforts in their Christian faith and practice, especially in their worship and song: "The greatest theologians have always refused to water down the gospel. Indeed, they have done the opposite—they have reminded us of the need for strenuous thinking, for a disciplined life of prayer, for a process of continually growing into the full maturity of Christ. . . . Such a theological position is not a brief against new music in the church. It is simply a call not to corrode and distort the strenuous quality of a life that for God risks everything."[127]

Many active churchgoers in this study rely almost exclusively on Sunday morning worship to shape their Christian lives and practice. Most members do not read the Bible either devotionally or critically and few pray other than occasionally before a meal and sporadically, as need arises. In his research, Wuthnow found: "The spiritual realm is a reality that people can muse about in everyday life, but its location remains on the periphery of their daily routines. It diverts little of their attention. It does not require them to set aside portions of their day to pray, worship, read sacred texts, reflect on ways to deepen their relationship with God, or be of service to others."[128] These observations are not intended so much to produce a wringing of hands or a pointing of fingers, but to sound a clarion call to the church that a life of Christian discipleship requires more of a believer than a casual commitment and requires more of a congregation than hoping members will learn to follow Christ through religious osmosis. Benton Johnson writes eloquently and persuasively on this issue: "Spiritual practice waters the roots of the soul and thereby enlivens the spirit. When done by members of a community, it recreates the energy to sustain its morality, which means that it is able to sustain both itself and its various missions. Without teaching and spiritual practice the will to live by the moral code of a faith fades away."[129]

Pastors and lay leaders can conduct many seminars on how to be productive and effective church managers, but more important, congregations need to see their leaders model a life of prayer.

Such a life of prayer, according to writer Anita Mathias, is "archaic, anachronistic, against the grain of modern life . . . it demands an expenditure of time that sometimes seems like a waste of time, a waste of self."[130] Throughout the Gospels, Jesus consistently "wastes" both time and self in prayer and then returns to the social demands upon him. He models for Christians and for the church that a life of prayer is not something extraneous to social involvement, but is foundational to it. In addition to modeling a life of prayer, Jesus also teaches his disciples to pray. Just as with devotional reading of the Bible, many members, especially members relatively new to Christian faith and practice, do not know the rubric for prayer, so they model what they see in popular culture. Congregations that do not model and teach the theology of and explain the rubric of a life of prayer will wither before the demands put upon the Christian faith today.

The church also needs to see its leaders model a discipline of devotional and critical reading of the Bible. We may well be living in a time in which deeply committed Christians and traditions cannot reach consensus with other Christians and traditions on how to read and best interpret scripture, but surely the church and its leaders can model a respect for scripture and an openness to the guidance of God's Spirit as we debate how, in the words of Douglas John Hall, we will *stand under* the Bible in order finally to *understand.* Pastors and educators, trained in biblical content, hermeneutics, and critical analysis are often strangely reluctant to share tools that uncover complexities within scripture. As long as they do not teach these tools to members, from fear that more conservative members might question their convictions or from fear that they might lose power by imparting specialized knowledge, they deprive members of a revelatory window into the mind of God. This task will also require that pastors and educators lower their swords and treat each other with respect.

The question then occurs: Are churches and their leaders up to such challenges? Louis Weeks, president of Union Theological Seminary and Presbyterian School of Christian Education, of the Presbyterian Church (U.S.A.), asks a series of directly related questions: "Pastors and educators continue to be called into service, but in a culture that awards authority for performance rather than for office, are they prepared sufficiently for leadership? . . . Are enough gifted men and women called into ministry today? . . . Are we demanding and supporting enough of institutions of secondary and higher education—and especially theological seminaries—to have them provide the training adequate for those who attend and learn there?"[131] A. James Rudin, national interreligious affairs director of the American Jewish Committee, cites similar concerns as Weeks: "Some young Protestants who reject the ministry cite the generally low pay of a pastor in an affluent society. They are put off by the long hours and seven-day workweeks constituting the usual work pattern of so many ministers, and believe they can serve God and their church as well as maintain a better family life without becoming a minister."[132]

A related question concerns growth in spiritual awareness that pastors and educators experience in their theological education. As people in and out of the church call for spiritual resources, many seminaries of mainline traditions have recently added everything from a chair of Spiritual Enrichment to an expectation that students will work with spiritual directors. Perhaps these trends may provide religious leaders who are better equipped to lead members into solitary or small group lives of disciplined study and prayer. However, some fear that the common concept of spirituality being nurtured in seminaries and then in congregations is too constrictive. Lynn and Wheeler quote a prominent denominational lay leader: "I would hope that seminaries would try to inculcate religious leaders with a sense that there is a civic dimension to the practice of religion in our country that is legitimate. [Clergy ought not just] be 'good girls and boys' and just minister to their communicants' needs and help them with their personal journeys through life. . . . If I have a message it would be, 'Train civically engaged leaders.' "[133] Congregations must insist that theological education prepare religious leaders who can model and teach a life of personal devotion and prayer. In addition, these leaders must be prepared to teach members to look inwardly only so long as to best discern how to be instruments of God's redemptive power in the world.

In the New Testament, a decision to follow Jesus as a disciple comes at a cost. In years past, when church and American culture were wed, discipleship and citizenship were largely indistinguishable and rarely costly. Civic loyalty supported church attendance and the church supported civic loyalty. This bond began to break in the latter decades of the twentieth century and the church of the twenty-first century may find itself increasingly estranged from the surrounding society.[134] People who will come to mainline congregations will often lack any but a superficial notion of personal piety and discipleship. Vibrant and vital congregations will recognize this trend and their leaders will spend the necessary time and resources to teach and model Christian faith and life in practice.[135]

An Invitation to Practice

About a life of devotion to God, the prophet Micah once spoke these unforgettable words: "You have heard it said what is good, but to do justice, to love kindness, and to walk humbly with your God" (Micah 6:8 NRSV). Another commonly quoted verse about faith in practice comes from the apostle Paul when he lists the inadequacy of knowledge, power, and sacrifice "if I have not love" (1 Cor. 13:1–3 NRSV). A biblically informed faith results in a life of thankfulness and grateful obedience, never content to confine devotion to God either to a private room or a packed sanctuary. A biblically informed faith seeks understanding and shapes the way we live.

As more people than ever come to church today with little exposure to Christian faith and church life, caring congregations will provide them with sound teaching and thoughtful worship, but also with safe and nurturing forums for faith talk. In these forums, people can talk about the Christian faith, draw upon faith lessons of others, and find encouragement to practice a life of faithful discipleship both in and out of the church.

Historically, faith talk has been far too one-directional in most mainline denominations, typically from pulpit to pew with little room for questions and discussion. When you read through the

Gospels, you see but a small sample of the questions that the life and teaching of Jesus generated. Disciples wanted to know what to do about the man healing people in Jesus' name, but who was not one of them. Peter wanted to know why Jesus kept up his morbid talk, and Thomas wanted to know how Jesus expected him to know the way.

Following Jesus then and now produces profound theological and ethical questions, such as: "What wisdom does the life and teaching of Jesus provide on issues of gun violence or capital punishment or economic disparity or fair labor practices? How can Jesus expect believers to forgive without limit? Will this not serve to support an abuser's behavior and leave those whom society traditionally victimizes even more victimized? Will Jesus lead me somewhere other than I would find just as easily by myself?" People who aim their lives in the way of Jesus also have practical questions, such as: "How are decisions made in the church and why do we worship the way we do and what music is worthy to praise God and how much is right to put in the plate and what difference does believing in the promises of God really make?"

Some of these questions are answered as worshipers discern God's word, but many questions of faith require an exchange of views in a safe and supportive, biblically and theologically sound environment. Drew University professor Janet Fishburn argues that pastors serve the church best when they support such small group learning and discussion. In addition, Fishburn argues that pastors are uniquely equipped and specially charged to interpret scripture to those asking faith questions and to teach others to do so: "The pastor, by example, teaches others how to lead a group in Bible study related to their lives and work together. As needed, the pastor also teaches leaders of various groups in the church to become responsible for leadership of informal worship by forming groups in which church members learn Bible study skills and prayer."[136]

In an earlier time, when Sabbath observance was more common than today and the content and practice of the Christian faith passed from generation to generation, there existed a more clearly defined time and locus, and also a familiarity with the practice of faith talk. Today, when Sabbath observance frequently consists of only sporadic attendance at a Sunday worship service, and people come to church often despite their family's preference, caring congregations and their leaders will create multiple settings in which members can pass on the faith to each other, talk about the struggles of discipleship, and reinforce a life given to a regular regimen of worship, study, practice, and prayer.

Critics of the church today are prone to focus on a time in the church's past when the practice of the faith was exemplary. One such idealized period for church life and practice in America was the 1950s. Robert Wuthnow, though, casts a pall upon this popular myth: "Despite the surge in popular piety, observers frequently cautioned that spirituality in the 1950s was superficial. . . . Critics noted that people went to religious services but did little during the week to express their faith at work or to carry principles of justice and charity from the pews to the poor in their communities. Herberg wrote that Americans displayed 'A religiousness with almost any kind of content or none, a way of sociability or "belonging" rather than a way of reorienting life to God.'"[137] Arguably, there is not a time in America's religious past when the church "got it right." And since this is the first time in our religious history when the church must define itself and carry out God's mission apart from the powerful props of a kindly culture, the church must not fear failing, but confidently wait on God's Spirit, and then be willing to explore new models of discipleship.

In the new millennium, vibrant and vital congregations will help believers and seekers in reorienting life to God. As budgets shrink, space between worshipers in the pews expands, and culture wars split the faithful few remaining, church leaders wring their hands, preach their damning diatribes, and weep over the apparent death of a declining church. A revitalized church, though, asks not what happened to the happy marriage of church and culture, but celebrates a new life for God's church. It celebrates those who are coming and who choose to stay and finds ways to equip them for a rich life of discipleship that quickly moves them deeper than the shallow waters of consumer Christianity. Genuine discipleship compels believers and congregations to notice what many members of society never notice and to speak out when silence is preferred.

Nile Harper points to several dynamic urban congregations in the United States that have done more than notice injustice in their midst. In the recent past, when the church enjoyed a more honored place in public perception, religious leaders could often nudge civic leaders to do the right thing for the public good. Today, the church is expected to know its place, not irritate neighbors, and either say something positive about the prevailing power structure or say nothing at all. Reluctant to stir negative attention, churches often reduce justice to charity in an attempt to provide for human need while largely ignoring factors that contribute to this need.

Harper describes distinctive ministries in urban congregations today that move the church into the arena of advocacy for social justice. He then rightly contends: "To have a vital Christian witness, urban congregations must go beyond acts of charity. They must go beyond the need to feel good about giving. What is most valuable is active partnership between oppressed people seeking to change the conditions of injustice, and other people who are willing to join in a common effort so that equity can be established. The most important gift urban congregations can give is the creation of relationships within which people of different backgrounds can learn to trust, respect, and work together. The creation of such a community is the foundation for the redevelopment of the church and the neighborhood."[138] Though both Harper and the current study focus almost exclusively on urban congregations, the call for congregations to act charitably and insist on justice for those in the greatest need sounds as loudly in the rural South as on the pavement of Brooklyn.

A vibrant and vital congregation either of fifty or five thousand members will refuse to peddle parochialism as the will of God, nor will it separate the secular from the spiritual. Norman Shanks tells of a window in the historic Benedictine abbey on the isle of Iona: "On the side of one of the windows . . . is carved a cat and a monkey, symbolizing respectively contemplation and action, both necessary to a life of spirituality and commitment."[139] Such an understanding of faith and practice will breathe God's fresh Spirit into believers and congregations, reminding them that the Christian life is far more than what happens within a glorious Gothic sanctuary. The Christian life is measured by how life is lived every minute in the watchful and redemptive sight of a loving God.

Closing Thoughts

If this book errs in posing a promising future for the church of Christ Jesus, good. The voices in this book echo the cries of a new church which God is bringing forth, about which we are now seeing only the first signs. A faithful posture for disciples in the emerging church is looking ahead. In response to complaints of untraditional behavior from disciples of John the Baptist about Jesus' disciples, our Lord responds: "No one sews a piece of unshrunk cloth on an old cloak, for the patch pulls away from the cloak, and a worse tear is made. Neither is new wine put into old wineskins; otherwise, the skins burst, and the wine is spilled, and the skins are destroyed; but new wine is put into fresh wineskins, and so both are preserved" (Matt. 9:14–17 NRSV). Fully confident in a God who is doing new things in our midst, the church can welcome all who walk through its doors and resist being timid about following Christ today when so many people choose not to. For when you look closely at the stories surrounding the crucifixion, to follow Jesus has always been, and most likely, will always be the bold alternative.

Appendix A

Questionnaire

Name: _____ Gender _____ Age _____

Address: (optional, include if you want a synopsis of the results)

Street address _____

City _____ State _____ Zip Code _____

E-mail address _____ Fax _____

Name of civic/social clubs to which you belong: _____

Years a member of this congregation: _____

Collective years an active member of any Presbyterian congregation _____

Year baptized: _____ Year confirmed/made profession of faith _____

On average, how many Sunday worship services do you attend over a three-month period: _____

How often do you celebrate the sacrament of the Lord's Supper/Communion/Eucharist? _____ weekly _____ monthly _____ seasonally

How often would you prefer to celebrate the sacrament of the Lord's Supper?

_____

How often do you pray?	How often do you read the Bible?
_____ multiple times per day	_____ daily
_____ daily	_____ once a week
_____ once a week	_____ infrequently
_____ infrequently	_____ never

I feel most like a disciple of Christ Jesus when:

_____

_____

Appendix B

Focus Group Questions

Preamble

Welcome and thank you for joining this study. Let me say a few words of introduction and background before we begin. I am asking the questions in the written questionnaire and the ones in our group experience because they speak to issues about which I wrestle every day as pastor, a Christian, and a Presbyterian. They are issues with which I have wrestled now for nearly twenty years since my ordination in 1980 in Wilmington, North Carolina. Throughout my years as a pastor in the PC(USA), my experience has been that pastors tend to talk to other pastors, theologians to other theologians, biblical scholars to other biblical scholars; all of whom then deliver their insights to church members. In this study, I am interested in hearing from lay persons about what it means to be a Christian, a Presbyterian, and an active member of a Christian congregation today.

So for the next ninety minutes, you and I will reflect on what it means to be a Presbyterian Christian at the close of this century. I will ask you a series of questions to which there are no indisputable, right answers in the back of some book or in the back of my head. I will ask the same series of questions to two other groups from this congregation and to members of five other vibrant and vital Presbyterian congregations across the country. The value of this study will increase with honest and candid reflections from each participant.

1. I'd like to begin by asking you to think about someone from this congregation whose Christian life you really admire. Without naming names, tell me what it is about their Christian life that you most admire.

2. Suppose a new neighbor of non-Christian background asked you to name two or three of the essentials to being a Christian, what would you say?

3. That same neighbor heard you mention that you are a Presbyterian. His next question to you then asks what are two or three of the essentials to being a Presbyterian Christian. What would you say?

4. I return home after church Sunday after Sunday to greet neighbors busy mowing grass, returning from golf or tennis, sitting on the porch sipping Starbucks and reading the *Post*. Each of these neighbors cares about our neighborhood and our nation; they work hard and love their families. Many are involved in civic associations and are committed to improving our world. But not one of these neighbors regularly worships. Yet you do. Why?

5. What is most meaningful to you about the worship experience at [church's name]?

6. I'd like a quick show of hands for this question. Would you be a member of this congregation even if it were not a Presbyterian congregation?

7. This is a two-part question. First, what does the word "spirituality" mean to you when you use it or when you hear other people use it? Second, how do you nurture your own spirituality, spiritual growth, religious devotion?

8. What are the spiritual resources to which you turn and then draw upon in times of need?

9. In what ways, if any, does your Christian faith influence how you live each day and the vocational choices you make?

10. Have you ever participated in such an interview about your Christian faith and life? How did it feel to participate in such an interview?

Notes

1. *Reformed Liturgy & Music* 33, no. 2 (1999): 41.
2. Wade Clark Roof, *Spiritual Marketplace: Baby Boomers and the Remaking of American Religion* (Princeton, N.J.: Princeton University Press, 1999), 128.
3. Ibid., 84.
4. See pages 1–14 of Douglas John Hall, *Why Christian?* (Minneapolis: Augsburg, 1998).
5. On page 84 of his article "The Future of Faith: Confessions of a Churchgoer," in the November 1999 edition of *The New Yorker,* novelist John Updike cites a study by Mark Chaves, a sociologist from the University of Arizona. Updike writes: "Attendance and membership have been drifting lower ever since the baby boomers, joining churches as they began to generate families, started to wander away again. Though for decades polls have pegged the number of regular churchgoing Americans at around forty per cent, Chaves claims that only twenty-eight per cent of Roman Catholics and fewer than one in five Protestants are in church on Sunday morning."
6. On pages 33–35 of his book *After Heaven: Spirituality in America since the 1950s* (Berkeley: University of California Press, 1998), Princeton sociologist Robert Wuthnow reports that church attendance and membership in the South still exceeds that of other regions of the United States and that certain ethnic enclaves in urban areas promote church involvement more than dispersed ethnic groups.
7. Hall, *Why Christian?* 136.
8. In a recent *Washington Post* article (Jan. 18, 2000), staff writer Hanna Rosin quotes from *Shopping for Faith* by Richard Cimino and Don Lattin. Contrary to the conclusions reached from my study, Cimino and Lattin look at Christians who do not come to church today and conclude: "In the new millennium, there will a growing gap between personal spirituality and religious institutions. Spiritu-

ality and religious faith are increasingly viewed as individual private matters with few ties to congregation and community."

9. Roof, *Spiritual Marketplace,* 36–37.
10. From Norman Shanks, *Iona: God's Energy* (London: Hodder & Stoughton, 1999), 31.
11. Ibid., 31–32.
12. Roof, *Spiritual Marketplace,* 37.
13. David Steward, "Why Do People Congregate?" in C. Ellis Nelson, *Congregations: Their Power to Form and Transform* (Atlanta: John Knox Press, 1988), 84.

Also see pages 67–89 of Barbara Wheeler, "Uncharted Territory: Congregational Identity and Mainline Protestantism," in Coalter, Mulder, and Weeks, *The Presbyterian Predicament* (Louisville, Ky.: Westminster/John Knox Press, 1990).

14. Hall, *Why Christian?* 14.
15. In a recent book review in *The Christian Century,* Louis Weeks, president of Union Theological Seminary and Presbyterian School of Christian Education, recounts a conversation familiar to most mainline religious leaders: "A seminary colleague recently observed that current students differ from those of the 1970s and 1980s. 'When I began to teach, students who did not come from Presbyterian families apologized. Now they brag—"I came from a Baptist-Catholic background, became Orthodox, was born again in InterVarsity, and now I'm Presbyterian." It's the born and reared who apologize now.' "
16. Roof, *Spiritual Marketplace,* 9–10.
17. On page 4 of his book *Iona: God's Energy,* Norman Shanks, leader of the Iona Community in Scotland, writes: "The Christian gospel is 'good news' precisely because it promises hope for all. Its message is that God's love embraces every human situation, that no individual is beyond the scope of God's grace, that in Jesus Christ is embodied the reality that all things are made new, and that God's kingdom, in all its fullness, is already breaking into our frail, flawed world."
18. In his book *Urban Churches, Vital Signs: Beyond Charity Toward Justice* (Grand Rapids: Wm. B. Eerdmans Publishing Co., 1999), Nile Harper describes the revitalizing role of public engagement by urban congregations: "In the past decade, many urban churches have moved beyond charity toward justice. They have acted to form networks and collaborative partnerships to change public policy and structures to create new and more just conditions in urban communities." See p. 297.
19. Hall, *Why Christian?* 123.
20. On page 51 of his book *After Heaven,* Princeton sociologist Robert Wuthnow gives an evocative depiction of current life in American

society: "Contemporary life is fluid, an ooze that seeps out in all
directions. It is hard to know where the center of a suburb is, hard to
feel centrally connected to an employer who is seldom seen, and
hard to sink roots for a family whose members come and go according to their own schedules."

21. Hall, *Why Christian?* 137.
22. Steward, "Why Do People Congregate?" 88.
23. Hall, *Why Christian?* 148.
24. Wuthnow, *After Heaven*, 134.
25. Updike, "The Future of Faith," 85.
26. Roof, *Spiritual Marketplace*, 50.
27. Shanks, *Iona: God's Energy*, 200.
28. In *After Heaven: Spirituality in America since the 1950s,* Wuthnow
    contrasts the relatively low worship participation at the close of nine-
    teenth and now twentieth century America with its pinnacle in the
    1950s and early 1960s. See pp. 30–32.

    In "The Future of Faith: Confessions of a Churchgoer," John
    Updike writes: "According to a 1999 study by Mark Chaves, a soci-
    ologist at the University of Arizona, belief in the afterlife is going up,
    even as church attendance drops" (p. 85).
29. In *After Heaven,* Wuthnow cites a study of urban church goers in the
    1950s who reported, on average, twenty-seven relatives with whom
    they were personally acquainted and who in most cases lived close
    enough to visit at least once in a while. The family, along with the
    church, provided a stable religious community for the average wor-
    shiper. Wuthnow goes on to describe the major sociological shift that
    has resulted in the geographical dislocation of average urban church-
    goers from most of their extended family and as a result worshipers
    often look to the church to fulfill a need for a stable and supportive
    religious community. See pp. 35–36.
30. On pages 84–85 of *Spiritual Marketplace,* Roof puts into context the
    worship tendencies among baby boomers. In his study he asked:
    "For you, which is most important: to be alone and to meditate, or to
    worship with others?" He continued: "The question was aimed at
    tapping the extreme form of an individualistic, self-focused
    approach to the sacred, recognizing of course that the two are not
    mutually exclusive. Half of the respondents answered that they pre-
    ferred to be alone, and another 18 percent said both were important
    . . . which means that two-thirds leaned toward a spiritual style with
    the emphasis on meditation and aloneness."
31. Harper, *Urban Churches, Vital Signs,* 3.
32. Eunuchs were specifically excluded from the sacred assembly
    because of their sexuality. They were castrated males (see Deut.
    23:1). Here Isaiah contrasts "eunuchs who keep my sabbath" to

those who are commonly assumed to be the religiously faithful in Israel. For more information on eunuchs in the Bible, see p. 285 of *Harper's Bible Dictionary.*

33. Walter Brueggemann, "Together in the Spirit, Beyond Seductive Quarrels," *Theology Today,* July 1999, 161.

34. Hall, *Why Christian?* 145.

35. In *Spiritual Marketplace,* 124, Wade Clark Roof reports: "Those of a liberal Protestant theological heritage continue to abandon their identities—a pattern quite pronounced since the mid-1960s. Both the magnitude and continuation of this downward trend signal the extent of this tradition's loss over the culture."

36. In this study, the liturgy for the participating congregations was remarkably similar, with the exception of the Fifth Avenue Presbyterian Church, which still uses an order of worship popular throughout Presbyterianism in the post-World War II period. This congregation also uses a pre–World War II hymnal despite the availability of two more recent versions since the end of the war.

37. Thomas Troeger, "For God Risk Everything: Reconstructing a Theology of Church Music," *Reformed Liturgy and Music* 33, no. 3 (1999): 6.

38. See Shanks, *Iona: God's Energy,* 130–31.

39. The post–World War II Presbyterian Church was fond of citing 1 Cor. 11:29 as both the reason for welcoming only older youth or adults to the Lord's Table and for observing the sacrament with limited frequency so as to provide adequate time for worshipers to do due diligence to their spiritual lives before communing.

40. In a recent letter in the Dec. 27, 1999–Jan. 3, 2000, edition of *The New Yorker* (p. 5), Christina Shankar of Chestnut Ridge, New York, writes: "I agree with John Updike that Christianity . . . Seems to be fading. Could that be because many denominations have diluted sacredness out of the faith? Church services have become hug-thy-neighbor group-therapy sessions, confirmation classes bear the moniker 'Deviating for Christ' in an effort to attract teenagers with 'cool' language, and important religious services, like those at Easter and Christmas, include bunnies and Santas. Where is the sense of awe—even the touch of fear—of the Divine that I felt in the cathedrals of Europe or the church of my youth? God seems to have become a benign friend on whom one can call when needed, and Christianity merely a long-distance carrier to make that call. No wonder so many of us search for more."

41. Douglas John Hall describes typical young congregants in American churches today: "They may be the children or grandchildren of loyal churchfolk, who out of respect for their progenitors feel some lingering connections with Christianity, or are caused by present-day experiences to reconsider 'religion.' They aren't fighting Christian-

ity, as many of my youthful contemporaries were doing forty years ago when churches were still very much part of the authority structure of our society. Rather, many young people today are far enough away from Christianity to be curious about it again. They don't know very much about it and they doubt much of what they think they know" (*Why Christian?* vii).

42. In this respect, active churchgoers today swim against a rising tide of inward and personal religious expression, according to a recent study conducted by University of California sociologist Wade Clark Roof. Roof argues: "If, as many social scientists argue, religion has to do with two major foci of concerns—personal meaning and social belonging—then most certainly it is around the first of these that religious energies revolve primarily today" (*Spiritual Marketplace*, 7).

43. Ibid., 42.

44. *Gnostic* and *gnosticism* are taken from a Greek word meaning "to know." Gnosticism was prominent in the Hellenistic thought of the world of the New Testament and early Christian centuries. Among its many tenets, gnosticism held that only those who knew the secret language of the cult could be included. See Van A. Harvey, *A Handbook of Theological Terms* (New York: Macmillan Co., 1964), 105.

45. Douglas John Hall argues: "It is my impression that the greatest misunderstandings of Christianity present in our American and Canadian context today are misunderstandings perpetuated by Christian bodies themselves. Today's apologists have to deal with simplistic, one-sided, and misleading representations of Christian belief and practice stemming from avowedly Christian sources" (*Why Christian?* 175).

46. Hall moves from a strong criticism of ultraconservative Christianity to an equally strong criticism of liberal/radical Christian thought. Arguing for the reclaiming of the Bible from the radical right and left, Hall writes: "What worries me about some liberal forms of Christianity, including some that detest the adjective 'liberal' and like to be thought 'radical,' is that it is so out of touch with the Christian tradition. Too much liberal Christianity, including a good deal of what passes for high Christian scholarship, seems ready to let the Scriptures go" (*Why Christian?* 176–77).

47. On pages 30–31 of his essay "The Restructuring of American Presbyterianism: Turmoil in One Denomination," in *The Presbyterian Predicament: Six Perspectives,* ed. Milton J Coalter, John M. Mulder, and Louis B. Weeks (Louisville, Ky.: Westminster/John Knox Press, 1990), Robert Wuthnow writes: "There is another kind of decline [in addition to a decline in membership] that may be even more indicative of the changes facing established religious bodies in our society. This is the decline of denominationalism. By all indications, Presbyterians have not only been diminishing in numbers but

have also experienced an erosion in the social and cultural boundaries that have set them off from other denominations in the past."

48. TULIP is an acronym originating in Dutch Calvinism. T stands for Total Depravity, the notion that nothing we do is exempt from the contaminating presence of sin. U stands for Unconditional Election, the notion that God will choose whomever God wills to choose. L stands for Limited Atonement, the notion that Christ died only for the Elect—those chosen by God for salvation. I stands for Irresistible Grace, the notion that no sinner, among the Elect, can ultimately stray from the saving grace of God. P stands for Perseverance of the Saints, the notion that God will sustain the chosen for all time.

49. The quotation, found on pages 285–86, is from *The Re-Forming Tradition,* a book in the research series titled *The Presbyterian Presence: The Twentieth Century Experience.* Authors Milton J Coalter, John M. Mulder, and Louis B. Weeks describe the project and resulting books in their series foreword: "Funded by the Lilly Endowment and based at Louisville Presbyterian Theological Seminary, the project is part of a broader research effort that analyzes the history of mainstream Protestantism" (see p. 14).

50. On pages 281–85 of *The Re-Forming Tradition,* Coalter, Mulder, and Weeks outline a set of theological questions that American Presbyterians and mainstream Protestants need to address in disestablished America.

51. On page 135 of his book *Why Christian?* Douglas John Hall makes this trenchant comment about wasting resources on a futile reclamation of Christendom: "Too many churches . . . are trying very hard to keep Christendom alive—to put that Humpty Dumpty together again. . . . But if they would give up on such a futile project and ask seriously about the alternatives that are open to them just at this point in time they might be filled with new enthusiasm and new life."

52. On pages 38–39 of Robert Wuthnow's article "The Restructuring of American Presbyterianism: Turmoil in One Denomination," in *The Presbyterian Predicament: Six Perspectives,* he writes: "Special purpose groups . . . resemble what sociologists have called 'struggle groups': that is, special interests organized specifically to engage in combat with other special interests, to champion their own cause, and to see their cause win over the hearts and minds of denominational officials."

53. In ibid., p. 32, Wuthnow writes: "It has . . . become easier for clergy trained in seminaries outside the denomination to be ordained. An estimated third of all Presbyterian clergy, for example, no longer receive training in the denomination's seminaries."

54. On page 17 of their collection of essays titled *The Presbyterian Predicament: Six Perspectives,* Coalter, Mulder, and Weeks wisely

warn the church today: "The loss in membership, a perceived spiritual malaise throughout much of the church, and the widely voiced perception that serious theology has not characterized the Presbyterian Church's recent history trouble the prospects for the church's future vitality."

55. See Wuthnow's book *After Heaven: Spirituality in America since the 1950s.*

56. Ibid., p. 1. Hanna Rosin, staff writer for *The Washington Post,* has an article in the January 18, 2000, edition titled "Beyond 2000: Many Shape Unique Religions at Home." She tells the story of Ed and Joanne, former Roman Catholics, who now are a church unto themselves. Rosin writes: "Now they commune with a new God, a gentle twin of the one they grew up with. He is wise but soft-spoken, cheers them up when they're sad, laughs at their quirks. He is, most essentially, validating, like the greatest of friends." Rosin quotes Joanne, who says: "We need God. Because we are God."

57. Roof, *Spiritual Marketplace,* 89.

58. The Rule of the Iona Community has five parts: a daily devotional discipline, an economic discipline for the sharing of and accounting for the use of money, a discipline of balancing the use of time, a social justice discipline of committing to actions of justice and peace, and a discipline of meeting regularly within the Community.

59. Shanks, *Iona: God's Energy,* 3–4.

60. On page 10 of *Spiritual Marketplace,* Roof states his thesis: "The boundaries of popular religious communities are now being redrawn, encouraged by the quests of the large, post-World War II generations, and facilitated by the rise of an expanded spiritual marketplace. The notion of a 'spiritual marketplace' is itself captivating, with the image of a quest culture shaped by forces of supply and demand, and of a remaking of religious and institutional loyalties."

61. Wuthnow, *After Heaven,* 3.

62. The contemporary confusion over the meaning of spirituality is reflected in *Webster's New World Dictionary,* where six definitions are offered for the word *spiritual.*

63. Shanks, *Iona: God's Energy,* 13.

64. Roof, *Spiritual Marketplace,* 109.

65. Wuthnow, *After Heaven,* 77.

66. Richard Cimino and Don Lattin, in *Shopping for Faith: American Religion in the New Millennium* (San Francisco: Jossey-Bass, 1998), write: "In the new millennium, there will be a growing gap between personal spirituality and religious institutions. . . . Spirituality and religious faith are increasingly viewed as individual private matters with few ties to congregation and community."

67. Douglas John Hall, *Thinking the Faith: Christian Theology in a North American Context* (Minneapolis: Augsburg, 1989), 285.

68. Wuthnow, *After Heaven,* 27.
69. In an appeal to a certain bloc of voters, political candidates will often appeal to the Bible as endorsing their particular position on an issue, but when pushed to cite biblical texts, they often expose a glaring ignorance of both biblical content and responsible interpretation.
70. On pages 2 and 7 of his book *Finally Comes the Poet: Daring Speech for Proclamation* (Minneapolis: Fortress Press, 1989), Walter Brueggemann writes: "To address the issue of a truth greatly reduced requires us to be poets that speak against a prose world. I shall continue to argue that the continuing practice of this artistic speech voiced in the prophetic construal of the Bible is the primary trust of the church and its preaching. This speech prevents our reduced world from becoming brutal and coldly closed upon us. This speech, entrusted to and practiced by the church, is an act of relentless hope; an argument against the ideological closing of life we unwittingly embrace." On pages 263–64 of his book *No Future without Forgiveness* (New York: Doubleday & Co., 1999), (now retired) Archbishop Desmond Tutu retells the Genesis story of the garden of Eden. He concludes: "This story is the Bible's way of telling a profound existential truth in the form of highly imaginative poetry. Prosaic, literal-minded spirits who cannot soar in the realms of the muse will be dismissive of this highly imaginative storytelling."
71. Hall, *Why Christian?* 176.
72. On page 265 of his book *No Future without Forgiveness,* Archbishop Tutu draws on a critical reading of scripture to make a remarkable announcement, given the horrors of the system of apartheid through which he had lived. Against biblicistic simplifiers who use the Bible to establish who is in and who is out, Tutu offers a more profound reading. He writes: "God has set in motion a centripetal process, a moving toward the center, toward unity, harmony, goodness, peace, and justice, a process that removes barriers. Jesus says, 'And when I am lifted up from the earth I shall draw everyone to myself' as he hangs from His cross with outflung arms, thrown out to clasp all, everyone and everything, in a cosmic embrace, so that all, everyone, everything, belongs. None is an outsider, all are insiders, all belong. There are no aliens, all belong in the one family, God's family, the human family. We are different so that we can know our need of one another, for no one is ultimately self-sufficient."
73. On page 36 of *Iona: God's Energy,* Shanks quotes Kenneth Leech from his book *The Eye of the Storm:* "Spirituality can be a dangerous diversion from the living God. It can be a form of illusion. Today 'spirituality' is marketed as a product, in competition with others, on

the station bookstalls. It belongs to the area of 'private life.' Of all the distortions of Christian faith and discipleship, it is individualism that has most penetrated spiritual consciousness."

74. Wuthnow, *After Heaven,* 105–6.
75. Coalter, Mulder, and Weeks, *The Re-Forming Tradition,* 263.
76. Shanks, *Iona: God's Energy,* 14.
77. On page 142 of *After Heaven,* Wuthnow explains: "Another important development that came to the late 1980s and 1990s was a renewed interest in the inner self as a way of relating to the sacred. . . . Readers were offered a beguiling mixture of therapeutic, recovery, and religious advice that would help create the kind of self needed to seek spirituality despite growing uncertainties about the nature of the sacred."
78. The apostle Paul nowhere more eloquently describes our interdependence with God and each other than in Galatians. He writes: "There is no longer any such thing as Jew and Greek, slave and free, male and female; for you are all one in Christ Jesus" (Gal. 3:28; au. trans.).
79. Shanks, *Iona: God's Energy,* 150.
80. Coalter, Mulder, and Weeks, *The Re-Forming Tradition,* 287.
81. Harper, *Urban Churches, Vital Signs,* 1.
82. Hall, *Why Christian?* 123.
83. Updike, "The Future of Faith," 86.
84. On page 42 of *Spiritual Marketplace,* Roof observes: "Many in these generations [those born after World War II] know very little about specific teachings, or how one faith community differs from another; many just nominally involved within churches, synagogues, and temples find it difficult to articulate what they believe."
85. On page 208 of his book *Generation to Generation: Family Process in Church and Synagogue* (New York: Guilford Press, 1985), rabbi and psychotherapist Edwin H. Friedman notes the healing impact when leaders in a congregation draw upon their faith to maintain a non-anxious presence: "Not only can such capacity [to maintain a nonanxious presence] enable religious leaders to be more clear-headed about solutions . . . but, because of the systemic effect that a leader's functioning always has on an entire organism, a nonanxious presence will modify anxiety throughout the entire congregation."
86. Robert Wuthnow, *The Restructuring of American Religion* (Princeton, N.J.: Princeton University Press, 1988), 265.
87. On page 128 of *Spiritual Marketplace,* Roof comments on the common search in America today for more enduring realities than economic ones: "Even among those lacking a good vocabulary for expressing their inner selves, or for whom spirituality is vaguely

defined and without much real power to challenge their secular values and assumptions, there is a yearning for something that transcends a consumption ethic and material definitions of success."

88. On page 198 of his book *After Heaven,* Robert Wuthnow contends: "The shift that has taken place in U.S. culture over the past half century . . . means that attention again needs to be given to specific spiritual practices by those who desire to live their whole lives as practice."

89. Frederick Buechner, *Wishful Thinking, A Seeker's ABC* (San Francisco: Harper, 1993), 58.

90. Shanks, *Iona: God's Energy,* 83.

91. Ibid., 221–22.

92. C. Ellis Nelson, *Congregations: Their Power to Form and Transform* (Atlanta: John Knox Press, 1988), 1.

93. Harper, *Urban Churches, Vital Signs,* 5–6.

94. On page 264 of their book *The Re-Forming Tradition,* Coalter, Mulder, and Weeks make an argument based upon a study of the Presbyterian Church (U.S.A.), but one that has clear parallels in most mainline denominations: "The Louisville research project points to an arresting conclusion about the PC(USA) as a denomination—namely, that the power and vitality of American Presbyterianism rests largely in congregations. As denominational structures have weakened, congregations are emerging as the key place where Christian faith and Presbyterian identity are forged and where diverse forms of mission take place."

95. On page 3 of his book *Five Challenges for the Once and Future Church* (Bethesda, Md.: Alban Institute, 1996), Loren B. Mead, founder of the Alban Institute, describes the changing role of national denominations in twentieth-century religious life in America: "The rich variety of national and regional church structures developed by 1960 were supported because thousands of local congregations knew in their bones that that was the way to support the mission that had been laid upon the church. The members of local congregations had a clear sense of what that mission was, and they supported it with some enthusiasm."

96. On pages 278–79 of their book *The Re-Forming Tradition,* Coalter, Mulder, and Weeks contend that conservative and liberal factions in the Presbyterian Church (U.S.A.) today are fighting the wrong enemy: "A recovery of theological vision in American Presbyterianism and mainstream Protestantism must begin with a mutual recognition by the contending parties in the internecine Protestant civil war that the threats each represent to the other are minor in comparison to the corrosive effects of secularity."

97. Mead, *Five Challenges for the Once and Future Church,* 16.

98. Ibid., 27.

99. Shanks, *Iona: God's Energy,* 211.

100. Ibid., 211.

101. Recall the observation of Mark Chaves (n. 5 above) that "only twenty-eight per cent of Roman Catholics attend Mass on a given weekend and fewer than one in five Protestants are in church on Sunday morning."

102. See pages 84–89 of Coalter, Mulder, and Weeks, *The Re-Forming Tradition;* see also page 42 of Roof, *Spiritual Marketplace.*

103. Raymond Schulte, "Creating Readiness: Who's Your Church?" in *Center Letter* 30, no. 2 (February 2000): 1.

104. Ibid.

105. Glenn McDonald, "Imagining a New Church," *Christian Century,* September 8–15, 1999, 854.

106. Nancy T. Ammerman, "New Life for Denominationalism," *The Christian Century* (March 15, 2000): 307.

107. In their book *Resident Aliens: Life in the Christian Colony* (Nashville: Abingdon Press, 1989), Duke scholars Stanley Hauerwas and William Willimon argue that the image of resident alien is an appropriate one for the church in a post-Christian culture.

108. Shanks, *Iona: God's Energy,* 205.

109. Roof, *Spiritual Marketplace,* 158.

110. Ibid., 128.

111. Harper, *Urban Churches, Vital Signs,* 298–99.

112. Coalter, Mulder, and Weeks, *The Re-Forming Tradition,* 201.

113. Ibid., 202.

114. *The Zacchaeus Project, A Ministry of The Episcopal Church Foundation* (Memphis, Tenn., 1999), 11.

115. Ammerman, "New Life for Denominationalism," 304.

116. On page 57 of *Spiritual Marketplace,* Roof writes: "Many people never exposed to a religious culture, or who dropped out of churches and synagogues when they were quite young, report that when they go to religious services they often feel awkward, not sure of what to say or how to act. Tensions often arise at baptisms and services of the Eucharist, because people are unsure of what the vows and symbols mean and whether or not it is hypocritical to participate if they are not fully committed to the faith."

117. Mead, *Five Challenges for the Once and Future Church.*

118. Elizabeth Lynn and Barbara G. Wheeler, "Missing Connections: Public Perceptions of Theological Education and Religious Leadership," *Auburn Studies,* no. 6 (September 1999): 1.

119. Ibid., 7.

120. McDonald, "Imagining a New Church," 852.

121. Ammerman, "New Life for Denominationalism," 302.

122. As quoted in Ammerman, "New Life for Denominationalism." © Copyright 1999, Garrison Keillor, Minnesota Public Radio.

123. Roof, *Spiritual Marketplace*, 11.

124. Wuthnow, *After Heaven*, 198.

125. Ibid.

126. Shanks, *Iona: God's Energy*, 137.

127. Thomas Troeger, "For God Risk Everything," 6–7.

128. Wuthnow, *After Heaven*, 134.

129. Benton Johnson, "Presbyterians and Sabbath Observance," in Coalter, Mulder, and Weeks, *The Presbyterian Predicament: Six Perspectives*, 107.

130. Anita Mathias, "Learning to Pray," *Christian Century*, March 22–29, 2000, 342.

131. Louis B. Weeks, "Speaking Honestly for a Faith that Endures," *As I See It Today*, winter 2000.

132. A. James Rudin, "As Spirituality Booms, Minister Shortage Deepens," *Presbyterian Outlook*, March 13, 2000, 9.

133. Lynn and Wheeler, "Missing Connections," 7.

134. On page 3 of his book *The Restructuring of American Religion*, sociologist Robert Wuthnow describes a huge parade in Brooklyn on June 6, 1946: "In the reviewing stand Brooklyn's mayor, the governor of New York, and a justice of the U.S. Supreme Court gave their approval. By public declaration all schools were closed for the day. . . . The event was the 117th annual Sunday School Union parade. Little more than a generation later, the world of the Brooklyn Sunday school parade seems strangely out of place. More than the differences in dress, or even the location, the idea of thousands of people turning out for a Sunday school parade taxes the imagination. That the event should enlist broad support from local officials and involve closing the public schools seems even less imaginable."

135. On page 851 of his article "Imagining a New Church," in the September 8–15 issue of *The Christian Century*, Glenn McDonald describes a major change in how his congregation understands its role as disciple-makers: "We set before the congregation the ideal of six marks of the disciple. These include a heart for Christ alone, a mind transformed by the word, arms of love, knees for prayer, a voice to speak the good news and a spirit of sacrifice."

136. Janet E. Fishburn, "Leading: Paedeia in a New Key," in C. Ellis Nelson, *Congregations: Their Power to Form and Transform* (Atlanta: John Knox Press, 1988), 216.

137. Wuthnow, *After Heaven*, 40.

138. Harper, *Urban Churches, Vital Signs*, 298–99.

139. Shanks, *Iona: God's Energy*, 143.